A VIETNAM EXPERIENCE

A VIETNAM EXPERIENCE

TEN YEARS OF REFLECTION

VICE ADMIRAL
JAMES B. STOCKDALE

HOOVER INSTITUTION

STANFORD UNIVERSITY, STANFORD, CALIFORNIA

The Hoover Institution on War, Revolution and Peace, founded at Stanford University in 1919 by Herbert Hoover, who went on to become the thirty-first president of the United States, is an interdisciplinary research center for advanced study on domestic and international affairs. The views expressed in its publications are entirely those of the authors and do not necessarily reflect the views of the staff, officers, or Board of Overseers of the Hoover Institution.

www.hoover.org

Section XIII from "Autumn Journal" reprinted by permission of Faber & Faber Ltd from *The Collected Poems of Louis MacNeice*.

Hoover Institution Press Publication No. 315
Hoover Institution at Leland Stanford Junior University,
Stanford, California, 94305-6010

First printing, 1984
26 25 24 23 22 21 20   25 24 23 22 21 19
Manufactured in the United States of America.
The paper used in this publication meets the minimum
Requirements of the American National Standard for
Information Sciences—Permanence of Paper for Printed
Library Materials, ANSI/NISO Z39.48-1992. ⊚

Library of Congress Cataloging-in-Publication Data
Stockdale, James B.
A Vietnam experience : Ten years of reflection.
    p. cm. — (Hoover Institution Press publication ; no. 315)
Includes bibliographical references and index.
ISBN-13: 978-0-8179-8151-8 (cloth : alk. paper)
ISBN-10: 0-8179-8151-9 (cloth : alk. paper)
ISBN-13: 978-0-8179-8152-5 (pbk. : alk. paper)
ISBN-10: 0-8179-8152-7 (pbk. : alk. paper)
    1. Naval art and science—Addresses, essays, lectures. 2. Military ethics—
Addresses, essays, lectures. 3. Stockdale, James B. 4. Admirals—United States—
Biography. 5. United States—Biography. 6. College presidents—United States—
Biography. I. Title.
VA50.S76 1984
359.0092'4 [B]—dc20   84-19349

Design by P. Kelley Baker

CONTENTS ⎯⎯⎯⎯⎯⎯⎯⎯⎯⎯⎯

FOREWORD

James B. Stockdale was a patriot and philosopher-warrior. His place in American history had been long secured, in part as someone who understood and loved history, closely studying and living the lessons passed to us from the ancients. As America again celebrated its independence and freedom the day prior to his passing in 2005, it provoked a time for Americans to celebrate him. He had borne the physical burdens of years of brutality at the hands of his Vietnamese captors; during his final years he endured the often equally brutal, long, slow march of Alzheimer's disease. The man who kept faith with his country and his comrades in arms; who, in what he saw as a debt of honor, underwent the harsh light of the political stage; who demonstrated that love and commitment can transcend the harshest circumstances; and who stayed true to his convictions even in the most painful and bitter moments was freed.

Vice Admiral Stockdale, a senior research fellow and honored colleague at the Hoover Institution, received national and worldwide attention during his time spent as a prisoner of war and subsequent release. More came to know him during his brief stint as Ross Perot's vice-presidential running mate, that view, however, as so many public snapshots, did not do justice to the man.

To know Admiral Stockdale's story is to know that brief moment in his and our lives was for him both an aberration and true to form. Many wondered why a man who shunned the public stage would take part in a national campaign, but those who knew him understood why he had taken on such an onerous task. When Perot—who had helped Stockdale, his fellow POWs, and their families during the bleakest parts of their lives—asked him to help fulfill his political aspirations, Stockdale felt that he could repay the debt only by agreeing to do so.

Rather than taking the easy way out—turning his back on a commitment, calling it quits, and trying to regain some semblance of a normal life (options similar to those offered by the Communists during his captivity and torture)—he hung in there. He kept the faith.

Thus it is difficult to understand how this Medal of Honor recipient, best-selling author, university president, scholar, and vice-presidential candidate would rate an obituary that was so "modest." One might have assumed his place in history would warrant greater attention and detail.

But for those of us who knew Admiral Stockdale, we can hear him counseling us to revisit the lessons of Epictetus's *The Enchiridion,* also known as *The Manual.* That ancient text strengthened and inspired him during his brutal seven-and-a-half-year imprisonment (four in solitary confinement; two in leg irons), interrogations, and torture sessions. In speeches and elsewhere, Admiral Stockdale extolled the virtues of a liberal education, discussing how the lessons he learned—including those from *The Enchiridion*—were the very ones that brought order, discipline, hope, and acceptance to the horrific confines of North Vietnam's Hoa Lo prison.

By relying on principles handed down by philosophers such as Epictetus and Seneca, he was able to make an impossible situation bearable. Admiral Stockdale's stoic calm in the midst of this man-made misery, helped him establish communication codes and a code of conduct for his fellow POWs. For his leadership of the prisoners' resistance efforts, his captors mercilessly tortured him again and again. And though they were able to break his body, they were not able to break his spirit.

At times, it must have seemed that Epictetus was speaking directly to his very conditions. Stockdale had injured his leg on ejecting from his crashing aircraft, and the North Vietnamese interrogators zeroed in on those wounds when it came time to deal out pain. The ongoing damage resulted in bouts of agony, fused his knee, and put a permanent hitch in his gait. Rather than sink into a spiral of self-pity, resentment, and anger, however, he called on the philosopher's (who was also lame) words: "Lameness is an impediment to the leg but not the will."

Admiral Stockdale would be the first to say that he was not a superman, able to had rise above the human condition or impervious to error. But he strove to learn from his experiences so that he might effect change—for the better—as he went along.

The first lesson of *The Enchiridion* provided one of his many pillars of strength, whether he was being brought to his knees by torturers or mocked by the pseudo-intelligentsia for his performance during the vice-presidential debates. Epictetus explained that some things are in our control and others are not. If something was out of your control, "be prepared to say that it is nothing to you."

Admiral Stockdale's ability to discern those things that are important was the hallmark of his character. Time and again, he was faced with adversities that would have broken many. But he was able to call on the wisdom and lessons of the past and rise above those conditions. Admiral Stockdale's life story, personal philosophy, and the lessons he passed on to us are not mysterious, difficult to find, or hard to remember. Living them out—in bad or good times—is the test.

It was a test James B. Stockdale passed with flying colors.

Admiral Stockdale's *A Vietnam Experience* has been one of the Hoover Press's most popular books since its first printing in 1984. This foreword, marking his passing in 2005, is the only revision to the original book.

> *Jeffrey C. Bliss*
> *Associate Director—Communications*
> *HOOVER INSTITUTION*
> *Stanford University*
> *Stanford California*

PREFACE _____

This is a piece of my life—my thoughts during the ten years after what was for me a ten-year war.

I first sailed into the waters off Vietnam as a carrier-based fighter pilot in the spring of 1963. Two and a half years later, on my third eight-month cruise there, I was shot down on a combat mission and taken prisoner. The date was September 9, 1965. I was ultimately released to go home in the spring of 1973.

The North Vietnamese prison where we American pilots were locked up was not a prisoner of war camp in the usual sense. It was a political prison. Political prisons are not for detention, for imposing punishment, or for preventing certain people from being at large. They are places where people are sent to be used for political purposes, or to have their minds changed, or both. These snake pits cast themselves as therapeutic rehabilitation centers, places where people get rid of antisocial tendencies. If the inmates are slow to pick up on the "suggested writings" cooked up by the political cadres, writings such as public confessions of error and guilt, then tourniquet-wielding torture specialists help them clear their minds. "Diehards" are kept in solitary confinement; I spent four years without seeing an American. The term of the sentence has nothing to do with the initial "crime." One is set free when the "treatment" has been completed, when the inmate is intimidated enough to freely spout the party line and "rejoice in his redemption," unless, of course, his sense of dignity and self-respect keeps him there till the drill is over, till the war has run its course.

Ninety-eight percent of us American pilots came out the latter way, the hard way. One *can* come out of an experience like that with a lot of the normal mental tangles of maturity all sorted out in the mind. As from political prisons of the past, a few Miguel de Cervanteses, Feodor Dostoyevskys, Arthur Koestlers, and Aleksandr Solzhenitsyns may have come out with us. We can't be sure yet. But there were many of us who were able to use the fire that was meant to destroy us as a saving fire, as a cauterizing agent, as a temperer of what became our steel.

In this book, chronologically arranged, are some of my writings, including inwspaper, magazine, and professional journal articles, plus a few public speeches that capture my reflections from spring 1973 to spring 1983. This ten-year span of time immediately following my ten years in the cauldrons of the Southeast Asia prison, saw me in a Navy hospital in San Diego; in a flying job as a Rear Admiral at sea out of San Diego; a single year (my only one in a 36-year career) in Washinton, D.C.; two years as Pre3sident of the Naval War College at Newport, Rhode Island; through navy retirement, then a year as president of a civilian college in Charleston, South Carolina; a winter of teaching at Hampden Sydney College in Virginia; and finally through the first two years of current appointment as a Senior Research Fellow at the Hoover Institution at Stanford.

James Bond Stockdale
The Hoover Institution
May 1984

ACKNOWLEDGMENTS _____

My thanks to my Hoover Institution colleague Richard Burress, who conceived of the idea of publishing this anthology; he made it happen with the help of the Hoover Institution Press. Jane Bavelas was the editor who sifted through ten times the number of articles you see below, selected these which frame the essence of my thoughts, and groomed them into proper book form. The conversion of all this material into a coherent manuscript was accomplished by my editorial assistant, Diane McAfoos Hydrean.

UNWINDING IN THE HOSPITAL

I. On my final combat cruise I was gone from San Diego just a few weeks short of eight years. At home in Coronado in the spring of 1965, I had left my wife, Sybil, and sons Jimmy (a high school freshman), Sid (fifth grade), Stan (a five-year-old preschooler), and Taylor (who had turned three just the day before I sailed). By the time they all met my plane on the ramp back in San Diego—on February 15, 1973—Stan and Taylor were "quite grown up" baseball players in the Coronado Little League, Sid was in his senior year of prep school in Connecticut, and Jimmy had finished college the previous spring.

After a loving private family reunion of a day or two, things commenced to steadily boil up to a way of life that neither Sybil nor I had predicted or liked: although I remained an outpatient at the local Navy Hospital, I was continually pressured into more public relations activities than I wanted to be involved in, and suddenly swamped with the Navy business of legal redress of a few, and the rehabilitation, promotion, and assignment of scores of men who had come out of the Hanoi prisons under my command. I had thought that somebody else would entertain the public, would have made themselves familiar enough with the details of our incarceration to take care of the follow-up required to set us back on course. But from the highest military and civilian ranks on down, it was strictly: "After you, Sir." "This is your project." "Not to tread on your toes, Sir." "What shall we do first, Sir?"

Soon Sid had to go back east to finish school, and the younger *boys naturally focused on the business of growing up at home in our happy town of Coronado. But Syb and Jimmy saw my need for administrative help and time to myself to unwind and put the past together. Jimmy stayed with me all that spring, getting me set up in an office at home, equipping me with papers and pencils and pens and books (things I had not seen for seven and a half years), while Syb performed stabilizing miracles of loving care and understanding.*

It was Jimmy who said: "You've got to take time out for yourself and do something that has some lasting importance and makes you feel good. Enough of this PR crap. Let's try to get something on paper about where you've really been." For about five days I relaxed and scribbled and flashed back to how it had been, years before, when little Jimmy and Sid would take the bus and come over to Yuma, Arizona, and stay with their Dad over the weekends when I was a Navy Commander in my thirties, commanding officer of a fighter squadron. (In those days I would spend seven days a week, six or eight weeks a year, over there in the desert shooting banner gunnery practice with my pilots.)

The result of this mixture of reflections on prison and how it was at home before I left was the following article. Jimmy called it in to the New York Times. *It appeared on the op-ed page of their Sunday edition on April 1, 1973. (This happened to be the very date on which my post-release promotion to Rear Admiral became effective.)*

BACK FROM HANOI _____

The New York Times, April 1, 1973

Ten years ago, I toured the old Yuma Territorial Prison with my two eldest sons. Then aged twelve and eight, they had come on the bus from San Diego the previous day to visit me. Our visits together were not frequent. I was the commanding officer of a Navy fighter squadron and much of my time was spent away from home either at sea or on the gunnery ranges in Arizona.

Their boyish reactions to the filthy cells used for solitary confinement were predictable. A blend of wonderment and horror crossed their faces as they peered in at the leg irons in the tiny, windowless concrete boxes. I assured my boys that the days of wild Western desperados, as well as jails such as these, were gone forever.

Yet I secretly shared their sense of terror. I could not imagine how the human spirit could maintain stability of purpose if shackled in these dark and dirty cells. The impact of the warm, dry afternoon was subtle. I had thought it an innocent enough excursion with perhaps a surreptitious lesson in humility for my sons.

It proved to be much more.

Within a few years I found myself in an old French-built isolated cell block in Hanoi. I was one of eleven Americans living in tiny, windowless concrete boxes (complete with leg irons) finding out firsthand the capabilities and limitations of the human spirit in such a situation. The abstract puzzle of a few years before had become a practical problem of daily survival. How could men maintain their senses of purpose and stability in an environment designed to break either or both?

We called our prison Alcatraz. Each of the inmates had a pedigree. Instead of horse theft or bank robbery, our "offenses" covered the full range of acts which might be considered resistance or opposition to the authority of our captors.

I was the senior officer in confinement there and believe I had the easiest leadership job in the world: to maintain the organization, resistance and spirit of ten of the finest men I have ever known. Each was his own man, with separate senses of purpose and stability, but with a common dedication to the military ethic. Pedantic arguments of international politics were wasted on us. We had a war to fight, and were committed to fighting it from lonely concrete boxes. Our very fiber and sinew were the only weapons at our disposal. I think we used them well.

It is not my purpose, though, to spout platitudes, nor do I seek the sympathy of the reader through recitation of what it is like to live in a quagmire of extortion, degradation, misery and pain. I address myself to the sorting and sifting for a common denominator which allowed those at Alcatraz, and scores of other prisoners of war with whom I have served, to return home with heads held high. A structured set of values supporting a basic tenet of self-respect was fundamental to the performance of these men.

My primary focus along these lines was acquired as a result of my association with Dr. Philip Rhinelander, a professor of philosophy at Stanford University. During my more difficult days in prison, I traced many of my needs for self-discipline to the readings he had assigned and tutoring he had given me during my postgraduate study. At our last private session, Dr. Rhinelander noted that I was a military man and for that reason gave me a copy of the *Enchiridion* by Epictetus. Epictetus was the son of a Roman slave, and this particular writing was what might be considered a manual for the combat officer of his time. I read it at home that evening and was puzzled. The format of classical stoicism was not new to me. But why had my professor chosen this reading as a parting gift? I was an organizer of men and a fighter pilot, concerned with the technology of the age. How could the foundations of the Aurelian stoical school apply to my daily life?

My question was answered in North Vietnam. When I ejected from that airplane in 1965, I left my world of technology and entered the world of Epictetus. I was alone and crippled; self-reliance was the basis for daily life. The system of values I carried with me into this realm was to be tested by my captors. The payoff was my self-respect. I would keep it or it would be torn from me and used as leverage against my senses of purpose and stability. I remembered the basic truth of subjective consciousness as the ability to distinguish what is in my power from that which is not. I recalled that "lameness is an impediment to the leg, but not to the will" and I knew that self-discipline would provide the balance I would need in this contest of high stakes.

These were the lessons of Epictetus and the core of my values or rules for survival. They served me well, and I walked out of Alcatraz with my self-respect. I know that the ten men there with me also walked out with their self-respect. Each man's values, from his own private sources, provided the strength enabling him to maintain his senses of purpose and dedication. Our value systems had in common the fact that they were based on rules, that they placed unity above self and that they precluded self-indulgence.

Each member of our "Alcatraz Gang" won his war from a filthy cell. Each man passed his own acid test. We were men under pressure at center stage in the drama of our era. Finally, most of us have come home. We do so with pride and joy. We return to a fast-paced America as neither a monolith of common opinion nor a cheap commercial commodity. The men of Alcatraz return home as individuals. To treat us as anything less is an injustice none of us deserves.

From the time I returned to the United States on February 15, 1973, throughout the rest of that year, I was attached to the Balboa Naval Hospital, San Diego. I had suffered serious untreated bone breaks in Vietnam: my left knee, vertebrae in my back, my left shoulder— all shattered. The Navy finally sent me to the Mayo Clinic for extensive consultations, and their doctors and I agreed that it was better to leave everything alone. By that time nature, without medical assistance, had worked nine years to make me a functional anthropoid. "You have stability, and you now have no pain," said the Mayo doctors. "Surgery would be exploratory, because we don't know where the blood vessels have routed themselves among the shattered bones." After hearing that, I gladly took Nature's stiff left leg and immobile left arm and went to Pensacola to take a flight physical. My friends the flight surgeons gave me a choice: immediate physical disability retirement or a "public relations OK" for flight. In other words, if I wanted to, I could fly the jets again. I wanted to, and was ordered to a flying job starting in January 1974.

But it was only the fall of 1973. Sid had finished prep school and entered college, Jimmy had gone back to Ohio to teach, and with Syb's help, I was trying to keep up with the rat race of naval courts and boards and public relations into which I had been plunged almost from the moment I had limped off the airplane the previous February. By then I had learned that audiences had nationally known prestige factors. And at the very pinnacle of prestige were a very few, large-city, influential membership, high-attendance luncheon clubs. I found myself in that circuit on October 19, 1973, when I spoke to The Executives' Club of Chicago. An abbreviated version of what I said appeared in the Congressional Record *the following May and is printed below.*

EXPERIENCES AS A
POW IN VIETNAM

Congressional Record, Proceedings and Debates of the 93rd Congress, Second Session, May 20, 1974. At the request of Senator Domenici.

The original speech was given for the Executives' Club, Chicago, Illinois, and was reprinted in *Executives' Club News*, vol. 50, no. 4.

Last February, when I first touched foot on American soil, I was asked to make a few remarks on behalf of the ex-POWs who were embarked in the airplane with me. An ancient verse came to mind that best summarized my relief at dropping the mantle of leadership and responsibility I had held during seven and a half years of imprisonment, four of them in solitary. These lines are attributed to Sophocles; I remember them well because of their modern ring: "Nothing is so sweet as to return from sea and listen to the raindrops on the rooftops of home."

Well, I was dreaming. I had forgotten that an old sea captain's job does not end when he anchors in home port.

My wife, Sybil, and I have a private joke. Before I returned she was advised by a Navy psychiatrist: "The fellow will probably make a quick readjustment to modern society if you will remember one rule for the first few months: Don't put him in decision-making situations." The reality of my post-confinement simply did not allow such an environment. In the past year I have probably made more important decisions than in any like period in my life.

Today I find myself truly back home. I am back with old friends, back in my native Middle West, and I have decided that this is my last public speech as an ex-POW. I have no ambition to become a professional ex-prisoner. As soon as I finish today, I am going down to my farm in Knox County for a couple of days, then to Colorado to spend the weekend with my second son, who is in college there, then back to San Diego. Next week I hope to check out of the hospital, and, hopefully, I will be ready for a good seagoing job.

Incidentally, before we were released by the North Vietnamese, I had occasion to be approached by other prisoners who were thinking about their careers. We were all more or less pessimistic about our future utility to our services. Not with any malice; it was just that we had been used to living that stoic life and faced up to the fact that there was a good chance that our service careers had been overcome by time.

We came home to find that the service was devoted to giving us every chance to regain that time. I am informed, as our Navy ex-POWs' duty assignments are made, and their orders are good, that each man has been given the personal attention his devotion to duty deserves.

As a theme for this audience, I will address the subject of how a group of middle Americans—average American guys who have chosen military life as a profession—survived in a POW situation and returned home with honor.

The conditions under which American POWs existed have changed radically since World War II. It is no longer a matter of simply being shot down in your parachute, going to a reasonably pleasant "Hogan's Heroes" prison camp, and sweating out the end of the war. At least it was not that way in Vietnam. In Vietnam the American POW did not suddenly find himself on the war's sidelines. Rather, he found himself on one of the major battlefronts—the propaganda battlefront.

Our enemy in Vietnam hoped to win his war with propaganda. It was his main weapon. Our captors told us they never expected to defeat us on the battlefield, but did believe they could defeat us on the propaganda front.

Unlike the World War II POW, who was considered a liability, a drain on enemy resources and manpower, the American POW in Vietnam was considered a prime political asset. The enemy believed that sooner or later every one of us could be broken to his will and used as ammunition on the propaganda front. Some of us might take more breaking than others, but all of us could be broken.

Thus, for Americans who became POWs in Vietnam, capture meant not that we had been neutralized, but that a different kind of war had begun—a war of extortion.

For the sane man there is always an element of fear involved when he is captured in war. In Vietnam the enemy capitalized on this fear to an extreme degree. We were told we must live by sets of rules and regulations no normal American could possibly live by. When we violated these rules and regulations, we gave our captors what they considered sufficient moral justification for punishing us—binding us in ropes, locking us in stocks for days and weeks on end, locking us in torture cuffs for weeks at a time, and beating us to bloody pulps. As we reached our various breaking points, we were "allowed" to apologize for our transgressions and to atone for them by "confessing our crimes" and condemning our government.

At this point you may be asking the question: Had the POWs received any training to prepare themselves for possible capture? The answer is yes, and it was based on two things that I have come to respect very, very much.

One was the taking of physical abuse. I think if you were to prepare yourself to be a prisoner of war, and I cannot imagine anybody going about that methodically, one should include a course of familiarization with pain. For what it is worth, I learned the merits of men having taken the physical abuse of body contact in sports. It is a very important experience; you have to practice hurting. There is no question about it.

Second, survival school was based on taking mental harassment. Also, I came out of prison being very happy about the merits of plebe year at the Naval Academy. I hope we do not ever dilute those things. You have to practice being hazed. You have to learn to take a bunch of junk and accept it with a sense of humor.

On the subject of education, beyond the scope of survival school, there is always the question: Do we need to start giving a sort of counterpropaganda course? Should we go into the political indoctrination business?

I am not very enthusiastic about that. I think the best preparation for an American officer who may be subjected to political imprisonment, is a broad, liberal education that gives the man at least enough historical perspective to realize that those who excelled in life before him were, in the last essence, committed to play a role. He learns that though it is interesting to speculate about the heavens and the earth and the areas under the earth and so forth, when it comes right down to it, men are more or less obliged to play certain roles, and they do not necessarily have to commit themselves on issues that do not affect that role.

Now, how does the average American—which is what the POW is—deal with his world? On a day to day basis, the POW must somehow communicate with his fellows. Together they must establish a viable set of rules and regulations to live by. We were military men. We knew we were in a combat situation and that the essential element of survival and success in a combat situation is military discipline. That meant isolated though we were from each other, we could not afford to live in a democracy. We had no choice but to live in a strictly disciplined military organization—if you will, a military dictatorship.

Our captors knew this as well as we did. Several members of Hanoi's Central Committee had spent long periods in confinement as political prisoners. They felt that we too were political prisoners. They held as their highest priority the prevention of a prisoner organization because they knew an organized body of prisoners could beat their system. If they were to get what they wanted from us, they had to isolate every American who showed a spark of leadership. They did so. They plunged many of us into a dark, solitary confinement that lasted, in some cases, for years.

For us the Code of Conduct became the ground we walked on. I am not aware that any POW was able, in the face of severe punishment and torture, to adhere strictly to name, rank, and serial number, as the heroes always did in the old-fashioned war movies, but I saw a lot of Americans do better. I saw men scoff at the threats and return to torture ten and fifteen times. I saw men perform in ways no one would have ever thought to put in a movie, and because they did perform that way, we were able to establish communication, organization, a chain of command and an effective combat unit. We lost some battles, but I believe we won the war.

In fact, I am not so sure we lost many battles. Unless you have been there, it is difficult to imagine the grievous insult to the spirit that comes from breaking under torture and saying something the torturer wants you to say. For example, "My government is conducting a criminal war. I am a war criminal. I bomb churches, schools, and pagodas." Does that sound silly to you? It does to me. But I and many others were tortured in ropes for that statement. The reason it was important to take torture for that statement was to establish the credibility of our defiance—for personal credibility—so that the enemy would know that they must pay a high price to get us into public statements if they ever could. Needless to say, in a POW situation, viable leadership is not possible without example. In a unit with good communication, almost everyone knows what everyone else is doing or not doing most of the time.

In short, what I am saying is that we communicated. Most of the time most of us knew what was happening to those Americans around us. POWs risked military interrogation, pain, and public humiliation to stay in touch with each other, to maintain group integrity, to retain combat effectiveness.

We built a successful military organization and in doing so created a counterculture. It was a society of intense loyalty—loyalty of men one to another; of rigid military authoritarianism that would have warmed the cockles of the heart of Frederick the Great; of status—with such unlikely items as years in solitary, numbers of times tortured, and months in irons as status symbols.

Most men need some kind of personal philosophy to endure what the Vietnam POWs endured. For many it is religion; for many it is patriotic cause; for some it is simply a question of doing their jobs even though the result—confinement as a POW—may not seem necessarily fair. For myself, it seemed that becoming a POW somewhere, someday, was a risk I accepted when I entered the Naval Academy. I think it is fair to say that most POWs—including, certainly, those who did not attend service academies—felt that same way. They accepted this as a risk they undertook when they took their oath as officers. To be sure, very few sat around bemoaning their fate, asking the heavens, "Why me?"

As POWs who were treated not as POWs but as common criminals, we sailed uncharted waters. The Code of Conduct was the star that guided us, although several of us are making recommendations for its modification, particularly in the area of a prisoner's legal status. The Code did not provide for our day to day existence; we wrote the laws we had to live by. We established means for determining seniority. We wrote criteria and provided mechanisms for relieving men of command for good and sufficient cause—and we used those mechanisms. We set a line of resistance we thought was within the capability of each POW to hold, and we ruled that no man would cross that line without significant torture. Thus, in effect, we ordered men to torture.

From what I have said here today, I think you can realize that as we prison leaders developed this organization, this unity, this mutual trust and confidence, the loyalty that permitted us to ask a guy to give his all sometimes, we acquired a couple of things. We acquired a lot of close friends, but in addition we acquired a constituency. Now life has to make sense to that constituency. And that constituency comes home and says to itself: You spoke with force of law, and at great personal pain and inconvenience I obeyed that law, and now I come home and no one seems interested in whether everybody obeyed it, or not.

What kind of a deal is that? This is not a personal grudge thing at all. I hope you all understand that.

I'm too closely involved to be objective on some of these issues. I'm often asked how I feel about amnesty. It is a complicated question; I appreciate and understand it. Thank goodness I'm not going to have to decide it. I don't resent amnesty—not personally—I simply don't have a position on the subject.

A couple of final comments: Self-discipline was vital to self-respect, which in turn is vital to survival and meaningful participation in a POW organization. Self-indulgence is fatal. Daily ritual seems essential to mental and spiritual health. I would do 400 pushups a day, even when I had leg irons on, and would feel guilty when I failed to do them. This ritual paid valuable dividends in self-respect, and, incidentally, I learned yesterday at Mayo Clinic that it also paid physical dividends.

I thank God for the other Americans I was imprisoned with. The respect one develops for others in a POW situation is really indescribable. I think it might be best illustrated with a story of something that happened once when I was in solitary and under extremely close surveillance. I was in dire need of a morale boost when two other POWs, Dave Hatcher and Jerry Coffee, sent me a note at great risk to themselves. I opened it and found written the complete poem "Invictus."

> Out of the night that covers me,
> Black as the Pit from pole to pole,
> I thank whatever gods may be
> For my unconquerable soul.

In our effort to survive and return with honor, we drew on the totality of our American heritage. We hope we added something to that heritage. God forbid that it should ever happen to other Americans—to your sons and grandsons and mine—but if it does, we hope our experience will help to guide them and will give them the heart and hope they will need.

☆   ☆   ☆   ☆   ☆

Admiral Stockdale is currently serving as Commander, Antisubmarine Warfare Wing Pacific.

THE
WAR COLLEGE
YEARS

II.   *After two and a half years in the aviation command job and a year in the Pentagon, I got the third star of a Vice Admiral and was ordered to become the President of the Naval War College at Newport, Rhode Island. That was where I belonged. High command of a peacetime military force was not for me. My natural inclinations and the practicalities of fate had shaped my drives toward those of a teacher.*

Although since I had been repatriated I had gone through the motions of presiding over peacetime operations and jumping through the right hoops in the Pentagon, in a true sense all that had been a big comedown from my professional experiences in Vietnam—first a squadron commander and then a wing commander airborne with my pilots in the flak, and finally for years boss of the prison underground in Hanoi. In those jobs under life and death pressure, what I said, what I did, what I thought, really had an effect on the state of affairs of my world. It was a real world, not a paper world. I had to convince real people, people with a certain independent freedom of action, that my ideas were good; being an actor-functionary in a drama of functionaries, all players being on predictable tracks, was tame fare by comparison.

I was glad to be back in the world of ideas. I wanted to teach people about war. I had been a ringside witness to the disaster of a nation trying to engage in war while being led by business-oriented systems analysts who didn't know anything about it.

The Naval War College of Newport, Rhode Island, was the first senior service college to be founded in America. Now over a hundred years old, its purpose is to give senior officers (colonels, Navy captains) a sabbatical from routine peacetime duties to study history, international politics, and associated subjects, to focus on war as a unique and crucial component of the human predicament. Its founders, Stephen Luce and Alfred Thayer Mahan, had the foresight to realize that peacetime military organizations need a permanent intellectual fountain of strategic insight and enrichment lest they become dominated by bureaucrats. By tradition, the Naval War College has civilian faculty members: historians, political scientists, and economists with teaching experience in the best universities in New England. As their team-teachers are selected bright and experienced military officers. The "students," professional military officers in their forties, take up residence in Newport, with their families, for a full school year.

The fall of 1977 found Syb and me in the lovely old colonial mansion that is the President's House, overlooking Narragansett Bay, Stan with us there as a day student in a local prep school, Taylor at Rumsey Hall school down in Connecticut, Sid in college in Colorado, and Jimmy, now married to Marina, teaching in a private school in Columbus, Georgia. My boss, Admiral Jim Holloway, Chief of Naval Operations, came up from Washington on a chilly October day to preside at the brief ceremony before student body and faculty as I took over. My remarks of that day appear below.

WAR AND THE
STUDY OF HISTORY _____

Change of Command Address, Naval War College, Newport,
Rhode Island, October 1977

It has been said that ". . . everything depends upon the person who stands in the front of the classroom. The teacher is not an automatic fountain from which intellectual beverages may be obtained. He is a witness to guide a pupil into the promised land; but he must have been there himself." This faculty has been there, and they hold the respect that goes with that qualification.

I spent this week with the Academic Department Heads. And, at the urging of Professor Phil Crowl, by way of preparation, I consulted The Oracle. If you remember Phil's article in the *Naval War College Review*, you will recall that his is not The Oracle of Delphi but The Oracle of Newport, Rhode Island, a man I can now call my predecessor, Alfred Thayer Mahan. I've studied lectures Mahan gave here nearly one hundred years ago—one given in the year 1888 right over here at Founders Hall in the third year of his first term as President; another given four years later in 1892, just after he came back for his second term as President, delivered here to my right in what was then the brand new Luce Hall. Besides their courtliness (they are always addressed to the "Gentlemen of the Navy," which I thought rather classy), one of the first things to strike you is the timelessness of these talks. Their content verifies the wisdom of the philosophy he institutionalized here. In my words, "that in the profession of arms, historic evidence indicates that the method of their employment is at least as important to victory as their design, and that the capstone of a mature officer's education should focus on style rather than hardware." In Mahan's words, "the great warrior must study history."

Mahan is not blindly dogmatic and he is openly distrustful of simplistic historic analogies. But he nevertheless believes that an educated man with sufficient classical background can often perceive recognizable trends in events that occasionally allow him "that quickness to seize the decisive features of a situation and to apply at once the proper remedy—a stroke which the French call *coup d'oeil*, a phrase for which I know no English equivalent." He explains that what he speaks of is a memory bank full of historic facts that, after a fashion, form distinctive and educational patterns. Example: in the late 18th Century, French armorers discovered a method of casting cannon barrels that not only improved their accuracy but made them much lighter. To the pedestrian officer the latter advantage was a convenience. But to the Corsican Corporal of Artillery with a sense of history, and more than a little genius, the change portended an entirely new and different utilization of the weapon. It was not to be towed slowly across the plains by oxen, but quickly across the Alps by horses. Forts were to be bypassed, firepower concentrated. What was to the man on the street a metallurgical convenience was to Napoleon a geopolitical event that led to the conquest of Europe. History is full of similar examples. In our age, what was to us a nuclear event was to Hyman Rickover quite a different thing.

Another of the timeless aspects of Mahan's lectures was the clear evidence of the pressures and crosscurrents concerning War College course content that he experienced even when this school was in its infancy, the world's first War College. Throughout his talks he's obsessed with the definitions of practicality and theoretical considerations. And he talks somewhat humorously of his contacts with friends in Washington when they ask him, as he steps out of the Army-Navy Club on a brisk evening, "Are you going back to the War College? Do you expect to have a session there?" "Yes," he answers. One of his senior friends then sneers, "Are you going to do anything practical this time?" Offended, Mahan replies with questions like "What do you mean by practicality?" and so on and so forth. This theme is woven throughout his lectures. The preoccupation is there, and it is clear that he was under pressure. This pressure can still be felt.

Now, subject to possible direction by my boss, Admiral Holloway, I would like to state that I plan to make no abrupt changes in the curriculum. I get a lot of mail on this subject, from everybody from old retired acquaintances to boyhood friends. One letter that I got from a boyhood friend a few days ago read in part as follows, ". . . on the subject of the College curriculum, you mentioned that you have been bombarded with conflicting advice. That cross will be yours to bear as long as you are there. My advice is that you ignore all of us and get on about your own business." That letter dated the 3rd of October 1977 and signed by Stansfield Turner.

So I do this afternoon get on about this business of educating our most promising mid-career officers. And I do so with a sense of mission and, in all honesty, with a very comfortable degree of self-confidence. For although it will take me a few months to get up to speed on all the disciplines taught here—and I think they are the right disciplines—each in my view has blind spots in critical areas vis-à-vis the nature of war itself. On the national scale, failure to account for this has cost us dearly in the recent past.

If I can firmly establish and illuminate to the students here the inevitable blindnesses of these particularized specialties or disciplines in which we must work—blindness to the psychological and subjective, as well as the objective totality of the human experience we call war—I think I will have done something for my country.

We have at times made assumptions that did not account for such facts as: (1) War is a serious business; (2) People get mad in war; (3) The laws of logic are valueless in bargaining under those circumstances; and so on. We, they, everybody should be assumed to be ready to throw proffered options in the face of the enemy. After all, their and our honor is at stake. A force at war can't feint and engage and disengage like an adagio dancer, and it's well to know that before you go into combat.

As the German soldier and philosopher Clausewitz has said, "War is nothing but a duel on a national scale." And I think a professional military man can learn some bad habits by leading a life that is totally devoted to orderly processes. Duels, or street fights, are not orderly processes. Yet they are very good analogies to war.

In short, I don't think there is anything new under the sun, or that we're seeing the dawn of any new age. I think we can be grossly misled by statements of some of the so-called defense intellectuals of the sort commonly appearing even now, in the post-Vietnam era. For example, I quote from a scholar in a recent issue of a highly respected journal. "Waging war is no different from any resource transformation process and should be just as eligible for the improvements in proficiency that have accrued elsewhere from technological substitution." My experience, and it has been rather recent, puts me back in old Clausewitz' camp. He said, "War is a special profession. However general its relation may be and even if all the male population of a country capable of bearing arms were able to practice it, war would still continue to be different and separate from any other activity which occupies the life of man." Another old warrior, William Tecumseh Sherman said, "War is cruelty and you can't refine it."

I think, faculty and students, that we are involved in an enterprise that deserves our best attention. And I am glad to address it with you.

☆

At the Naval War College I had my own press that put out, among many other things, a periodical to a wide professional officer and national security academic audience: The Naval War College Review. I always wrote a short lead article for that under the title "Taking Stock." I also found myself being invited to make dozens of speeches—commencement speeches at civilian colleges, sermons at local churches, talks to professional societies. Then there were magazine articles. And all this was in addition to institutional affairs and classroom teaching, which I soon took up.

Below, in chronological order—at least in terms of time of composition—are an assortment of all of the above. Within a week of the time I took over the President's job it was time to compose the piece below for the Winter NWC Review.

TAKING STOCK ——————————————————————

Naval War College Review, Winter 1978

I was both surprised and pleased during my first week as President of the Naval War College, to have had so many of those well-wishers who stopped in or phoned include in their remarks comments on the *Naval War College Review*. Many friends—active and retired officers, congressmen, educators, and others—closed our conversations with "keep the *Review* coming." Not all its articles escape critical comment, but that is hardly surprising. This quarterly publication is not a house-organ, cranking out a particular party line, but a scholarly journal intended to stimulate and challenge its readers and to serve as a catalyst for new ideas.

I disagree with both the thrust and conclusions of some of the *Review*'s articles myself but my opinions do not necessarily detract from the value of those compositions. For instance, in this issue I take exception to Professor Hitchen's writing on the Code of Conduct. The subject is, of course, very close to me and I have read countless articles about, and heard many proposals for, revising the Code. His is what I might call the outsider's viewpoint; shared by many, it focuses on Article V (". . . I am bound to give only name, rank, service number, and date of birth.") as a flawed stipulation requiring revision. It has been my observation that those who have not served as prisoners of war but who write on such matters invariably assume that Article V is the "heart" of the Code. My further observation is that few of those who have been prisoners of war for a significant period of time have any trouble understanding or dealing with it. The Article is just a piece of good advice: to utter as little as possible except for the four items required under international law, at least until one is sufficiently certain of his ground to be able to use his words as weapons against his captors. That's what Brig. Gen. S. L. A. Marshall meant when he wrote it, and that's what it says.

If Article V was flawed, it was given clearer meaning in a Presidential Executive Order signed in November 1977. However, scarcely noted by commentators, a second, more important Executive Order was also signed at that time. That one dealt with Code provisions that have great significance for "insiders"; it dealt with command authority within a prison camp. The Code says that if one is senior he will take command and, that if not senior, he will obey the orders of the senior prisoner and back him up in every way. The shocking discovery for us who returned from North Vietnam was to be told that the Code did not have the force of law. Had this fact been generally known in prison, I'm afraid our POW military organizations would have been much less effective. Now that the cat is out of the bag, President Carter's new Executive Order should go far toward remedying what could have been a serious problem in the next war. As for Professor Hitchen's question: "Is the Code of Conduct required at all?," I believe that the answer is "no" for about 60 percent of the American fighting men. However, some of us need its moral support to hitch up our courage, and a few of us need a little fear of the law to keep it hitched up.

Institutional nepotism aside, I thought Captain Platte's multipolarity article was the finest in this issue. However, he isn't immune from disagreement either. He believes the U.S.S.R. best suited by experience to play the *balancer* in a tripolar world. I would argue that China is equally experienced. The Chinese Communists' World War II performance in fighting two enemies simultaneously, alternately siding with each against the other, must have set a record for aplomb and agility. At any rate, the true nature of their conflicts was certainly smoked by the man on the street in the United States. Americans, Captain Platte and I agree, will have the least affinity for three-cornered confrontations. Visualizing all the bad guys on one side and all the good guys on the other will never get us by.

I don't intend these notes merely to be a rebuttal or even a comment on every article. Rather, I intend to use this space as a sounding board to float a few ideas of my own.

In his *Nicomachean Ethics*, Aristotle, differing with his teacher Plato, held that although both are dear to us, piety requires that we honor truth even before our friends. I address this to my friends the strategists, the analysts, and the tacticians. The truth to be honored is that your analyses, your equations, your principles, and your plans too often are based on incomplete if not erroneous assumptions about the nature of man and the nature of war. The extension of rational management principles to planning and waging a war is obviously not without value. Indeed, to ignore those tools is crippling and criminally dangerous. Equally dangerous, however, is the belief that the uncritical application of those principles will bring victory in war. War is an irrational undertaking and there are no tenets of rationality to which all men subscribe. We may cry with Job, "Oh that mine adversary had written a book" but he hasn't and yet we err in ascribing our own values, reactions, cultural processes, etc., to him. This "mirror imaging" is often warned against but as often forgotten. It is a blind spot or perhaps more properly, a false view, a mirage, that we must rid ourselves of. We must do it nationally and we are going to do it in our courses of instruction here at the War College. In a future issue of the *Review* I wish to look into some specific aspects of this subject.

In the first article of this issue, The Honorable Edward Hidalgo warns that striving to avoid error is not the same thing as seeking the attainment of a positive goal—that avoiding failure is not success. I intend that my term as President of the Naval War College be devoted to the quest for the positive goal, but that will require good judgment. It has been said that good judgment is based on experience, but that, unfortunately, good experience is based on bad judgment. Once upon a time I zigged when I should have zagged. At any rate—

> The old order changeth, yielding place to new,
> And God fulfills himself in many ways,
> Lest one good custom should corrupt the world.
> —Alfred Lord Tennyson

My second NWC Review *article finally broached the subject that had been in my craw ever since my years spending my life locked in leg-irons on a cement slab bunk in central Hanoi listening to the carnival-like joyful noises in the streets outside just before and just after the surprise-free "daily air raids" McNamara's Pentagon Whiz Kids meticulously scheduled. These dinky raids were manifestations*

of their naive idea that delicate, tacit peacemaking signals could be transmitted by military action. Clausewitz would have choked. Did they not know his dictum? "War is an act of violence *intended to compel our opponent to fulfill our will." America was treating a serious subject, war, like a business school classroom exercise.*

TAKING STOCK ————————————

Naval War College Review, Spring 1978

Oscar Wilde once wrote that "Man is a rational animal who always loses his temper when he is called upon to act in accordance with the dictates of reason." He was not writing about war, of course, but his observation seems pertinent to one of our blind spots when thinking about and planning for war. We plan; we calculate; we consider and accept or reject options; we apply the most theoretically sound principles to our studies and we do it all in a rigorously rational way but whether through design or ignorance we too often forget that while war as political theory may be perfectly rational, warfare in practice is most decidedly not. Clausewitz said it this way: War is a trinity with its rational element being outweighed two to one by the combined elements of chance ("within which the creative spirit is free to roam") and blind natural force ("primordial violence, hatred and enmity"). I believe with Livy that the event corresponds less to expectation in war than in any other case whatever.

War never has been nor will be fought without Wilde's men who lose their temper and somehow their familiar rational processes are insufficient or inappropriate to the irrational game being played. I emphasize familiar lest it be incorrectly inferred that I have no brief for reason. Of course I do, but I think that reason must be expanded to include the subjective element, the man element—why he fights, how he fights, whether he must fight.

This is not a new question. Philosophers, real and fancied, have long grappled with it. One of them, an acquaintance and sometime correspondent of mine, recently died. He never taught at a military school or service college. As far as I know, he never made a study of war but he did study men in war. He received his doctorate in philosophy from Columbia University the same week he was called up in a pre–World War II draft. Eligible for a commission, he preferred to serve first as a foot-soldier, then as a counter-intelligence operative in Europe. His name was J. Glenn Gray. He kept a journal and copies of letters he wrote to his friends and in them he recorded his thoughts and observations of men in war. More than a decade after the war he put his reflections, then matured, into a book, *The Warriors*.

I disagree with Professor Gray in many particulars—at least I interpret some things differently—and I am not going to review his book here but I do commend it to all thoughtful readers. He writes in moving and literate prose of the paradoxes of man in war, the ecstasies and agonies, the glories of battle, the ugliness of death, the feelings of guilt and hate and rage, and the tremendous power of comradeship. It is all useful to an understanding of ourselves and of our adversaries. In my change of command address I noted that war is a serious business, that people get mad in war, and that the laws of logic are valueless in bargaining under such conditions. Gray helps us to see why.

One result of failure to accommodate psychological or subjective factors in our wishful thinking is that to which I referred in the last issue of the *Review*—perceptions and misperceptions. We delude ourselves in many things but one which is especially troubling to me and which I have had the opportunity of observing from another side is our attribution of our own characteristics and expected stimuli-responses to our adversaries. We plan and conduct elaborate and subtle operations intended to "signal" something to that adversary and are amazed at his response (or lack of same). We ignore or reply gently to aggressive provocation intending thereby to signal that we want to live in peace and harmony and are baffled when provocation increases. We gradually increase the power of our response in an attempt to signal our capability, our restraint, and our desire to give our opponent an out and are baffled that he, instead, lashes back in anger and vengeance. We mount a massive attack signalling determination, if little else, and are baffled that our opponent sues for peace. But why? Why should we be baffled? How much experience do we need? The results of our misapprehended signals are not hidden. I thought of this often as I lay in my cell in Hanoi and listened to the explosions of "measured U.S. response" signalling, by restraint, the American belief in the futility of continued North Vietnamese intransigence and hearing the contemptuous response of the jailers, the people in the street—we're angry, we don't want an out, we want to fight. And I stood with scores of American POWs and cheered while unmistakable commitment was registered as B-52 bombs thundered into military targets all night, night after night in late 1972, and felt the collapse of an enemy's will as those same jailers became apologetic and solicitous, and those same streets—well clear of the drop zones—fell silent. "Burning bridges behind us," not "keeping options open," squelched the war whoops of Hanoi.

There is a language of war, but it can't be faked. To win, it is necessary to understand it. It has long been clever to quote Clemenceau's belief that war is too important to be left to the generals. He may have been correct but the generals—and admirals and commanders and colonels—who are called on to conduct war had best know what they're about. And that's what we at the Naval War College are about.

THE NAVY AND NATIONAL STRATEGY

Opening Remarks, Annual Current Strategy Forum, Naval War College, Newport, Rhode Island, March 27, 1978

My name is Jim Stockdale; I had the good fortune to come here as President about six months ago. To give you a better handle on who I am, you should know that I've always wanted to be a schoolmaster. I like the academic environment, particularly when the subject matter involves institutions and issues dear to my heart, like a Navy which has been my home and life for 35 years, and like a country which I love very much—one which I want to see survive and prosper. So coming here has truly been an answer to my prayers. I like the give and take, the scrimmage of the classroom, and will commence conducting courses personally next term.

That's who I am, and I think I have a pretty good idea of who you are. As I've studied your distinguished backgrounds, I've seen names that I've admired from afar for years, and others belonging to people who have been near and dear to me during the most important times of my life. Among you are (now) civilian businessmen who were Naval and Marine officers with me as postgraduate students, destroyer sailors and fighter pilots. There are in this audience active duty officers who shared my exciting days as a test pilot and others who shared my even more exciting days as a prisoner of war. There are college professors here whom I have known as Carrier Landing Signal Officers and as classroom mentors, past and present.

So I welcome you all. It's the time of year when we gather together a widely representative group of American citizens—all with different backgrounds, different interests, different professions, different faiths, different disciplines, and certainly different convictions—but Americans all, and all concerned about how this Republic fares.

We're here for two days to focus on the subject, "The Navy and National Strategy: What Kind of a Future Navy and Why?" This is a very basic issue, one which I hope we can avoid obscuring with programmatic gobbledegook. It's a basic issue first because it's about force and power—national power. I know some of you abhor that subject, but I think it's regrettably true that war is the way of the world.

I once asked my favorite scholar of history, Will Durant, what he thought of our American foreign policy. (You'll notice I've been vague about when we talked and thus leave open the issue of what Administration was in power.) When Will Durant understood the question, he said, "Ah, I think we're all mixed up; we seem to be working on the assumption that if we're nice to other people they'll be nice to us. I can tell you that in the last 4000 years there's practically no evidence to support that view."

If you don't like the Durants' view of the utility of power, perhaps you will accept the way my predecessor, Alfred Thayer Mahan, saw it. "The purpose of power," said Mahan, "is to permit moral ideas to take root." I think that given the realities of this contentious world, there's a lot of truth in his statement.

The subject of the Navy and national strategy is basic, particularly for Americans, for a second reason. It concerns the sea and we Americans are children of the sea. Now it is true that from platforms such as this it is often specified on the first day that this is an island nation and that for commercial and other reasons we behave like an island. Or, as Henry Kissinger said a little more eloquently from this platform about two weeks ago, our history may be seen in three segments vis-à-vis the sea: first we saw the sea as a moat of protection, then as a haven for our ally—the British and their navy which protected us. And finally now it threatens to become a lair for our enemies with their missile submarines. But I mean we in America are children of the sea for much deeper reasons which have to do with the intellectual history and the cosmology of the Western mind. Because, you see, America was not discovered, it was invented.

Last Saturday night I spent all too many hours reading a fascinating book written 20 years ago by a Latin American scholar named Edmundo O'Gorman. Its title is *The Invention of America*. In well-footnoted detail he describes the terrible upheavals in scientific and religious thought set off by Christopher Columbus' cruise reports in the late fifteenth and early sixteenth centuries. Admiral Columbus was not much help in calming these upheavals because he clung to the myth that he had got to Asia. He made four cruises, and he patched together more or less the same rationalizations after each one. His arrival in Asia had become an obsession with him, a matter of faith, in spite of evidence he was clearly too intelligent not to recognize. But you see he had been paid to go to Asia, and his reputation was staked on the issue. He was *not*, as is commonly said, on the outs with Amerigo Vespucci. (Amerigo's early western explorations overlapped Christopher's later ones.) By a tacit agreement, Amerigo ultimately announced the truth, that there was a new continent, when it was polite to do so.

I want to talk a little more about these upheavals in scientific and religious thought. Columbus' claim that he arrived in Asia after so short a trip drove the mathematicians up the wall. Of course we all know that educated Westerners, way back to the Greeks, had known that the world was round; they also had a very good idea of how large it was. This half-size world of Columbus was throwing off all their astronomy calculations. Furthermore, Columbus' hypothetical world would have had to be mostly land. Science, folklore and religion had all, for centuries, held that the world was mostly water. All three turned out to be correct, of course. In the Book of Genesis, if you will remember, God parted the waters and made the earth. The earth was the exception. He created a world of islands, not a world of lakes. Western man grew up with great awe of the power of the sea. The Old Testament God was also a strict disciplinarian and He combatted evil with mighty weapons—with hordes of locusts, with famine, with drought, with pestilence. But after His Flood, even He had second thoughts, and went on record agreeing never to repeat it.

Theologians had many problems with a new continent. They had Adam and Eve problems, original sin problems. In those days there was a well-established "island of the earth" theory. Even St. Augustine's celestial city was open only to residents of Europe, Asia and Africa. In other words, Columbus raised some very delicate problems and we should be thankful that we did not have instant news analysis then as now or there would have been a lot of very disturbed people around. In the ways of the venerable institutions of those years a measured accommodation was made. It took fifteen years, but in 1507, one of the most important documents in geographic science appeared: "The Introductory Cosmology" by the Academy of St. Die. (That title is my translation of O'Gorman's Latin.) This document said that although the land was still divided into three parts (Europe, Asia and Africa), there was a fourth *special* part of the world. It was something like an island, something like a continent, but special, and called America, after its only discoverer with enough credibility left to lend it his name. Thus, the term "new world" which emerged with this document had deep symbolic meaning. It did not refer merely to some distant location which might be profitable for economic development or exciting for residence. The "new world" concept had much more impact on human minds than would result today, say in case of the discovery of a new celestial body, or resulted yesterday, say in the landing of the astronauts on the moon.

Why all this about intellectual history? Because we live in our minds, reality to each of us is largely what we want to believe. The reality of the association of the sea and the United States is that it has driven our history—not only our military and diplomatic history, but every brand of our history—our intellectual history, our economic history. One of dozens of seldom cited examples of the latter is the great change a single seaport brought to this country in the early nineteenth century. In the year 1820, the records tell us that slavery was all but dead in America. Its economic utility was drying up. So also drying up at an alarming rate was the very economy of the nation. The final successful cure for the latter originated in the minds of the traders of the great port of New York. They collaborated with the agronomists of the South and launched an industry that kept the country going for decades. That industry was cotton. Throughout that nineteenth century America grew cotton, grew cotton, and grew cotton—and always exported most of it to Europe. Now this had many effects. Plantations grew, slavery grew, Indian tribes were kicked off valuable lands in Alabama, the industrial revolution of the North was spurred, the nation was rent by a Civil War, a postwar capital and credit system grew in the great Northern cities, and so on and on. But it was our great seaports that made the difference, kept us alive, and gave us our unique American vitality, and all the good and all the bad that comes with it.

And so I say, is it not reasonable that we Americans, we men of this special place, this fourth place, this new world, very likely come by our national defense concept of a forward strategy naturally? What is more consistent with our cosmology, our self-image of differentness, our centuries-old habits of aloofness, than our tradition of keeping our ramparts at our adversaries' gates rather than at our shores?

Maybe we naturally assume we own the sea. Can we afford to give it up? Should we make ourselves afford it for the protection of our grandchildren?

THE WORLD OF EPICTETUS: REFLECTIONS ON SURVIVAL AND LEADERSHIP

The Atlantic Monthly, April 1978

In 1965 I was a forty-one-year-old commander, the senior pilot of Air Wing 16, flying combat missions in the area just south of Hanoi from the aircraft carrier *Oriskany*. By September of that year I had grown quite accustomed to briefing dozens of pilots and leading them on daily air strikes; I had flown nearly 200 missions myself and knew the countryside of North Vietnam like the back of my hand. On the ninth of that month I led about thirty-five airplanes to the Thanh Hoa Bridge, just west of that city. That bridge was tough; we had been bouncing 500-pounders off it for weeks.

The September 9 raid held special meaning for *Oriskany* pilots because of a special bomb load we had improvised; we were going in with our biggest, the 2000-pounders, hung not only on our attack planes but on our F-8 fighter-bombers as well. This increase in bridge-busting capability came from the innovative brain of a major flying with my Marine fighter squadron. He had figured out how we could jury-rig some switches, hang the big bombs, pump out some of the fuel to stay within takeoff weight limits, and then top off our tanks from our airborne refuelers while en route to the target. Although the pilot had to throw several switches in sequence to get rid of his bombs, a procedure requiring above-average cockpit agility, we routinely operated on the premise that all pilots of Air Wing 16 were above average. I test-flew the new load on a mission, thought it over, and approved it; that's the way we did business.

Our spirit was up. That morning, the *Oriskany* Air Wing was finally going to drop the bridge that was becoming a North Vietnamese symbol of resistance. You can imagine our dismay when we crossed the coast and the weather scout I had sent on ahead radioed back that ceiling and visibility were zero-zero in the bridge area. In the tiny cockpit of my A-4 at the front of the pack, I pushed the button on the throttle, spoke into the radio mike in my oxygen mask, and told the formation to split up and proceed in pairs to the secondary targets I had specified in my contingency briefing. What a letdown.

The adrenaline stopped flowing as my wingman and I broke left and down and started sauntering along toward our milk run target, boxcars on a railroad siding between Vinh and Thanh Hoa, where the flak was light. Descending through 10,000 feet, I unsnapped my oxygen mask and let it dangle, giving my pinched face a rest—no reason to stay uncomfortable on this run.

As I glided toward that easy target, I'm sure I felt totally self-satisfied. I had the top combat job that a Navy commander can hold and I was in tune with my environment. I was confident—I knew airplanes and flying inside out. I was comfortable with the people I worked with and I knew the trade so well that I often improvised variations in accepted procedures and encouraged others to do so under my watchful eye. I was on top. I thought I had found every key to success and had no doubt that my Academy and test-pilot schooling had provided me with everything I needed in life.

I passed down the middle of those boxcars and smiled as I saw the results of my instinctive timing. A neat pattern—perfection. I was just pulling out of my dive to the ground when I heard a noise I hadn't expected—the "boom boom boom" of a 57-millimeter gun—and then I saw it just behind my wingtip. I was hit—all the red lights came on, my control system was going out—and I could barely keep that plane from flying into the ground while I got that damned oxygen mask to my mouth so I could tell my wing-man that I was about to eject. What rotten luck. And on a milk run!

The descent in the chute was quiet except for occasional rifle shots from the streets below. My mind was clear, and I said to myself, "five years." I knew we were making a mess of the war in Southeast Asia, but I didn't think it would last longer than that; I was also naive about the resources I would need in order to survive a lengthy period of captivity.

The philosopher Durants said that culture is a thin and fragile veneer that superimposes itself on mankind. For the first time I was on my own, without the veneer. I was to spend years searching through and refining my bag of memories, looking for useful tools, things of value. The values were there, but they were all mixed up with technology, bureaucracy, and expedi-ency, and had to be brought up into the open.

Education should take care to illuminate values, not bury them amongst the trivia. Are our students getting the message that without personal integ-rity intellectual skills are worthless?

Integrity is one of those words which many people keep in that desk drawer labeled "too hard." It's not a topic for the dinner table or the cock-tail party. You can't buy or sell it. When supported with education, a person's integrity can give him something to rely on when his perspective seems to blur, when rules and principles seem to waver, and when he's faced with hard choices of right or wrong. It's something to keep him on the right track, something to keep him afloat when he's drowning; if only for practical rea-sons, it is an attribute that should be kept at the very top of a young person's consciousness.

The importance of the latter point is highlighted in prison camps, where everyday human nature, stripped bare, can be studied under a magnifying glass in accelerated time. Lessons spotlighted and absorbed in that labora-tory sharpen one's eye for their abstruse but highly relevant applications in the "real time" world of now.

In the five years since I've been out of prison, I've participated several times in the process of selecting senior naval officers for promotion or im-portant command assignments. I doubt that the experience is significantly different from that of executives who sit on "selection boards" in any large hierarchy. The system must be formal, objective, and fair; if you've seen one, you've probably seen them all. Navy selection board proceedings go some-thing like this.

The first time you know the identity of the other members of the board is when you walk into a boardroom at eight o'clock on an appointed morn-ing. The first order of business is to stand, raise your right hand, put your left hand on the Bible, and swear to make the best judgment you can, on the basis of merit, without prejudice. You're sworn to confidentiality regarding all board members' remarks during the proceedings. Board members are chosen for their experience and understanding; they often have knowledge of the particular individuals under consideration. They must feel free to speak their minds. They read and grade dozens of dossiers, and each candidate is discussed extensively. At voting time, a member casts his vote by selecting and pushing a "percent confidence" button, visible only to himself, on a console attached to his chair. When the last member pushes his button, a totalizer displays the numerical average "confidence" of the board. No one knows who voted what.

I'm always impressed by the fact that every effort is made to be fair to the candidate. Some are clearly out, some are clearly in; the borderline cases are the tough ones. You go over and over those in the "middle pile" and usually you vote and revote until late at night. In all the boards I've sat on, no inference or statement in a "jacket" is as sure to portend a low confidence score on the vote as evidence of a lack of directness or rectitude of a candidate in his dealings with others. Any hint of moral turpitude really turns people off. When the crunch comes, they prefer to work with forthright plodders rather than with devious geniuses. I don't believe that this preference is unique to the military. In any hierarchy where people's fates are decided by committees or boards, those who lose credibility with their peers and who cause their superiors to doubt their directness, honesty, or integrity are dead. Recovery isn't possible.

The linkage of men's ethics, reputations, and fates can be studied in even more vivid detail in prison camp. In that brutally controlled environment a perceptive enemy can get his hooks into the slightest chink in a man's ethical armor and accelerate his downfall. Given the right opening, the right moral weakness, a certain susceptibility on the part of the prisoner, a clever extortionist can drive his victim into a downhill slide that will ruin his image, self-respect and life in a very short time.

There are some uncharted aspects to this, some traits of susceptibility which I don't think psychologists yet have words for. I am thinking of the tragedy that can befall a person who has such a need for love or attention that he will sell his soul for it. I use tragedy with the rigorous definition Aristotle applied to it: the story of a good man with a flaw who comes to an unjustified bad end. This is a rather delicate point and one that I want to emphasize. We had very very few collaborators in prison, and comparatively few Aristotelian tragedies, but the story and fate of one of these good men with a flaw might be instructive.

He was handsome, smart, articulate, and smooth. He was almost sincere. He was obsessed with success. When the going got tough, he decided expediency was preferable to principle.

This man was a classical opportunist. He befriended and worked for the enemy to the detriment of his fellow Americans. He made a tacit deal; moreover, he accepted favors (a violation of the Code of Conduct). In time, out of fear and shame, he withdrew; we could not get him to communicate with the American prison organization.

I couldn't learn what made the man tick. One of my best friends in prison, one of the wisest persons I have ever known, had once been in a squadron with this fellow. In prisoners' code I tapped a question to my philosophical friend: "What in the world is going on with that fink?"

"You're going to be surprised at what I have to say," he meticulously tapped back. "In a squadron he pushes himself forward and dominates the scene. He's a continual fountain of information. He's the person everybody relies on for inside dope. He works like mad; often flies more hops than others. It drives him crazy if he's not liked. He tends to grovel and ingratiate himself before others. I didn't realize he was really pathetic until I was sitting around with him and his wife one night when he was spinning his yarns of delusions of grandeur, telling of his great successes and his pending ascension to the top. His wife knew him better than anybody else; she shook her head with genuine sympathy and said to him: 'Gee, you're just a phony.'"

In prison, this man had somehow reached the point where he was willing to sell his soul just to satisfy this need, this immaturity. The only way he could get the attention that he demanded from authority was to grovel and ingratiate himself before the enemy. As a soldier he was a miserable failure, but he had not crossed the boundary of willful treason; he was not written off as an irrevocable loss, as were the two patent collaborators with whom the Vietnamese soon arranged that he live.

As we American POWs built our civilization, and wrote our own laws (which we leaders obliged all to memorize), we also codified certain principles which formed the backbone of our policies and attitudes. I codified the principles of compassion, rehabilitation, and forgiveness with the slogan: "It is neither American nor Christian to nag a repentant sinner to his grave." (Some didn't like it, thought it seemed soft on finks.) And so, we really gave this man a chance. Over time, our efforts worked. After five years of self-indulgence he got himself together and started to communicate with the prisoner organization. I sent the message "Are you on the team or not?"; he replied, "Yes," and came back. He told the Vietnamese that he didn't want to play their dirty games anymore. He wanted to get away from those willful collaborators and he came back and he was accepted, after a fashion.

I wish that were the end of the story. Although he came back, joined us, and even became a leader of sorts, he never totally won himself back. No matter how forgiving we were, he was conscious that many resented him—not so much because he was weak but because he had broken what we might call a gentleman's code. In all of those years when he, a senior officer, had willingly participated in making tape recordings of anti-American material, he had deeply offended the sensibilities of the American prisoners who were forced to listen to him. To most of us it wasn't the rhetoric of the war or the goodness or the badness of this or that issue that counted. The object of our highest value was the well-being of our fellow prisoners. He had broken that code and hurt some of those people. Some thought that as an informer he had indirectly hurt them physically. I don't believe that. What indisputably hurt them was his not having the sensitivity to realize the damage his opportunistic conduct would do to the morale of a bunch of Middle American guys with Middle American attitudes which they naturally cherished. He should have known that in those solitary cells where his tapes were piped were idealistic, direct, patriotic fellows who would be crushed and embarrassed to have him, a senior man in excellent physical shape, so obviously not under torture, telling the world that the war was wrong. Even if he believed what he said, which he did not, he should have had the common decency to keep his mouth shut. You can sit and think anything you want, but when you insensitively cut down those who want to love and help you, you cross a line. He seemed to sense that he could never truly be one of us.

And yet he was likable—particularly back in civilization after release—when tension was off, and making a deal did not seem so important. He exuded charm and hail fellow sophistication. He wanted so to be liked by all those men he had once discarded in his search for new friends, new deals, new fields to conquer in Hanoi. The tragedy of his life was obvious to us all. Tears were shed by some of his old prison mates when he was killed in an accident that strongly resembled suicide some months later. The Greek drama had run its course. He was right out of Aristotle's book, a good man with a flaw who had come to an unjustified bad end. The flaw was insecurity: the need to ingratiate himself, the need for love and adulation at any price.

He reminded me of Paul Newman in *The Hustler*. Newman couldn't stand success. He knew how to make a deal. He was handsome, he was smart, he was attractive to everybody; but he had to have adulation, and therein lay the seed of tragedy. Playing high-stakes pool against old Minnesota Fats (Jackie Gleason), Newman was well in the lead, and getting more full of himself by the hour: George C. Scott, the pool bettor, whispered to his partner: "I'm going to keep betting on Minnesota Fats; this other guy [Newman] is a born loser—he's all skill and no character." And he was right, a born loser—I think that's the message.

How can we educate to avoid these casualties? Can we by means of education prevent this kind of tragedy? What we prisoners were in was a one-way leverage game in which the other side had all the mechanical advantage. I suppose you could say that we all live in a leverage world to some degree;

we all experience people trying to use us in one way or another. The difference in Hanoi was the degradation of the ends (to be used as propaganda agents of an enemy, or as informers on your fellow Americans), and the power of the means (total environmental control including solitary confinement, restraint by means of leg-irons and handcuffs, and torture). Extortionists always go down the same track: the imposition of guilt and fear for having disobeyed the rules, followed in turn by punishment, apology, confession, and atonement (their payoff). Our captors would go to great lengths to get a man to compromise his own code, even if only slightly, and then they would hold that in their bag, and the next time get him to go a little further.

Some people are psychologically, if not physically, at home in extortion environments. They are tough people who instinctively avoid getting sucked into the undertows. They never kid themselves or their friends; if they miss the mark they admit it. But there's another category of person who gets tripped up. He makes a small compromise, perhaps rationalizes, and then makes another one; and then he gets depressed, full of shame, lonesome, loses his willpower and self-respect, and comes to a tragic end. Somewhere along the line he realizes that he has turned a corner that he didn't mean to turn. All too late he realizes that he has been worshiping the wrong gods and discovers the wisdom of the ages: life is not fair.

In sorting out the story after our release, we found that most of us had come to combat constant mental and physical pressure in much the same way. We discovered that when a person is alone in a cell and sees the door open only once or twice a day for a bowl of soup, he realizes after a period of weeks in isolation and darkness that he has to build some sort of ritual into his life if he wants to avoid becoming an animal. Ritual fills a need in a hard life and it's easy to see how formal church ritual grew. For almost all of us, this ritual was built around prayer, exercise, and clandestine communication. The prayers I said during those days were prayers of quality with ideas of substance. We found that over the course of time our minds had a tremendous capacity for invention and introspection, but had the weakness of being an integral part of our bodies. I remembered Descartes and how in his philosophy he separated mind and body. One time I cursed my body for the way it decayed my mind. I had decided that I would become a Gandhi. I would have to be carried around on a pallet and in that state I could not be used by my captors for propaganda purposes. After about ten days of fasting, I found that I had become so depressed that soon I would risk going into interrogation ready to spill my guts just looking for a friend. I tapped to the guy next door and I said, "Gosh, how I wish Descartes could have been right, but he's wrong." He was a little slow to reply; I reviewed Descartes's deduction with him and explained how I had discovered that body and mind are inseparable.

On the positive side, I discovered the tremendous file-cabinet volume of the human mind. You can memorize an incredible amount of material and you can draw the past out of your memory with remarkable recall by easing slowly toward the event you seek and not crowding the mind too closely. You'll try to remember who was at your birthday party when you were five years old, and you can get it, but only after months of effort. You can break the locks and find the answers, but you need time and solitude to learn how to use this marvelous device in your head which is the greatest computer on earth.

Of course many of the things we recalled from the past were utterly useless as sources of strength or practicality. For instance, events brought back from cocktail parties or insincere social contacts were almost repugnant because of their emptiness, their utter lack of value. More often than not, the locks worth picking had been on old schoolroom doors. School days can be thought of as a time when one is filling the important stacks of one's memory library. For me, the golden doors were labeled history and the classics. The historical perspective which enabled a man to take himself away from all the agitation, not necessarily to see a rosy lining, but to see the real nature of the situation he faced, was truly a thing of value.

Here's how this historical perspective helped me see the reality of my own situation and thus cope better with it. I learned from a Vietnamese prisoner that the same cells we occupied had in years before been lived in by many of the leaders of the Hanoi government. From my history lessons I recalled that when metropolitan France permitted communists in the government in 1936, the communists who occupied cells in Vietnam were set free. I marveled at the cycle of history, all within my memory, which prompted Hitler's rise in Germany, then led to the rise of the Popular Front in France, and finally vacated this cell of mine halfway around the world ("Perhaps Pham Van Dong lived here"). I came to understand what tough people these were. I was willing to fight them to the death, but I grew to realize that hatred was an indulgence, a very inefficient emotion. I remember thinking, "If you were committed to beating the dealer in a gambling casino, would hating him help your game?" In a pidgin English propaganda book the guard gave me, speeches by these communists about their prison experiences stressed how they learned to beat down the enemy by being united. It seemed comforting to know that we were united against the communist administration of Hoa Lo prison just as the Vietnamese communists had united against the French administration of Hoa Lo in the thirties. Prisoners are prisoners, and there's only one way to beat administrations. We resolved to do it better in the sixties than they had in the thirties. You don't base system-beating on any thought of political idealism; you do it as a competitive thing, as an expression of self-respect.

Education in the classics teaches you that all organizations since the beginnning of time have used the power of guilt; that cycles are repetitive; and that this is the way of the world. It's a naive person who comes in and says, "Let's see, what's good and what's bad?" That's a quagmire. You can get out of that quagmire only by recalling how wise men before you accommodated to the same dilemmas. And I believe a good classical education and an understanding of history can best determine the rules you should live by. They also give you the power to analyze reasons for these rules and guide you as to how to apply them to your own situation. In a broader sense, all my education helped me. Naval Academy discipline and body contact sports helped me. But the education which I found myself using most was what I got in graduate school. The messages of history and philosophy I used were simple.

The first one is this business about life not being fair. That is a very important lesson and I learned it from a wonderful man named Philip Rhinelander. As a lieutenant commander in the Navy studying political science at Stanford University in 1961, I went over to philosophy corner one day and an older gentleman said, "Can I help you?" I said, "Yes, I'd like to take some courses in philosophy." I told him I'd been in college for six years and had never had a course in philosophy. He couldn't believe it. I told him that I was a naval officer and he said, "Well, I used to be in the Navy. Sit down." Philip Rhinelander became a great influence in my life.

He had been a Harvard lawyer and had pleaded cases before the Supreme Court and then gone to war as a reserve officer. When he came back he took his doctorate at Harvard. He was also a music composer, had been director of general education at Harvard, dean of the School of Humanities and Sciences at Stanford, and by the time I met him had by choice returned to teaching in the classroom. He said, "The course I'm teaching is my personal two-term favorite—The Problems of Good and Evil—and we're starting our second term." He said the message of his course was from the Book of Job. The number one problem in this world is that people are not able to accommodate the lesson in the book.

He recounted the story of Job. It starts out by establishing that Job was the most honorable of men. Then he lost all his goods. He also lost his reputation, which is what really hurt. His wife was badgering him to admit his sins, but he knew he had made no errors. He was not a patient man and demanded to speak to the Lord. When the Lord appeared in the whirlwind, he said, "Now, Job, you have to shape up! Life is not fair." That's my interpretation and that's the way the book ended for hundreds of years. I agree with those of the opinion that the happy ending was spliced on many years later. If you read it, you'll note that the meter changes. People couldn't live with the original message. Here was a good man who came to unexplained grief, and the Lord told him: "That's the way it is. Don't challenge me. This is my world and you either live in it as I designed it or get out."

This was a great comfort to me in prison. It answered the question "Why me?" It cast aside any thoughts of being punished for past actions. Sometimes I shared the message with fellow prisoners as I tapped through the walls to them, but I learned to be selective. It's a strong message which upsets some people.

Rhinelander also passed on to me another piece of classical information which I found of great value. On the day of our last session together he said, "You're a military man, let me give you a book to remember me by. It's a book of military ethics." He handed it to me, and I bade him goodbye with great emotion. I took the book home and that night started to read it. It was the *Enchiridion* of the philosopher Epictetus, his manual for the Roman field soldier.

I had entered the world of Epictetus, and it's a world that few of us, whether we know it or not, are ever far away from.

In Palo Alto, I had read this book, not with contentment, but with annoyance. Statement after statement: "Men are disturbed not by things, but by the view that they take of them." "Do not be concerned with things which are beyond your power." "Demand not that events should happen as you wish, but wish them to happen as they do happen and you will go on well." This is stoicism. It's not the last word, but it's a viewpoint that comes in handy in many circumstances, and it surely did for me. Particularly this line: "Lameness is an impediment to the body but not to the will." That was significant for me because I wasn't able to stand up and support myself on my badly broken leg for the first couple of years I was in solitary confinement.

What attributes serve you well in the extortion environment? We learned there, above all else, that the best defense is to keep your conscience clean. When we did something we were ashamed of, and our captors realized we were ashamed of it, we were in trouble. A little white lie is where extortion and ultimately blackmail start. In 1965, I was crippled and I was alone. I realized that they had all the power. I couldn't see how I was ever going to get out with my honor and self-respect. The one thing I came to realize was that if you don't lose your integrity you can't be had and you can't be hurt. Compromises multiply and build up when you're working against a skilled extortionist or a good manipulator. You can't be had if you don't take that first shortcut, of "meet them halfway," as they say, or look for that tacit deal, or make that first compromise.

Bob North, a political science professor at Stanford, taught me a course called "Comparative Marxist Thought." This was not an anticommunist course. It was the study of dogma and thought patterns. We read no criticisms of Marxism, only primary sources. All year we read the works of Marx and Lenin. In Hanoi, I understood more about Marxist theory than my interrogator did. I was able to say to that interrogator, "That's not what Lenin said; you're a deviationist."

One of the things North talked about was brainwashing. A psychologist who studied the Korean prisoner situation, which somewhat paralleled ours, concluded that three categories of prisoners were involved there. The first was the redneck Marine sergeant from Tennessee who had an eighth-grade education. He would get in that interrogation room and they would say that the Spanish-American War was started by the bomb within the Maine, which might be true, and he would answer, "B.S." They would show him something about racial unrest in Detroit. "B.S." There was no way they could get to him; his mind was made up. He was a straight guy, red, white, and blue, and everything else was B.S.! He didn't give it a second thought. Not much of a historian, perhaps, but a good security risk.

In the next category were the sophisticates. They were the fellows who could be told these same things about the horrors of American history and our social problems, but had heard it all before, knew both sides of every story, and thought we were on the right track. They weren't ashamed that we had robber barons at a certain time in our history; they were aware of the skeletons in most civilizations' closets. They could not be emotionally involved and so they were good security risks.

The ones who were in trouble were the high school graduates who had enough sense to pick up the innuendo, and yet not enough education to accommodate it properly. Not many of them fell, but most of the men that got entangled started from that background.

The psychologist's point is possibly oversimplistic, but I think his message has some validity. A little knowledge is a dangerous thing.

Generally speaking, I think education is a tremendous defense; the broader, the better. After I was shot down my wife, Sybil, found a clipping glued in the front of my collegiate dictionary: "Education is an ornament in prosperity and a refuge in adversity." She certainly agrees with me on that. Most of us prisoners found that the so-called practical academic exercises in how to do things, which I'm told are proliferating, were useless. I'm not saying that we should base education on training people to be in prison, but I am saying that in stress situations, the fundamentals, the hardcore classical subjects, are what serve best.

Theatrics also helped sustain me. My mother had been a drama coach when I was young and I was in many of her plays. In prison I learned how to manufacture a personality and live it, crawl into it, and hold that role without deviation. During interrogations, I'd check the responses I got to different kinds of behavior. They'd get worried when I did things irrationally. And so, every so often, I would play that "irrational" role and come completely unglued. When I could tell that pressure to make a public exhibition of me was building, I'd stand up, tip the table over, attempt to throw the chair through the window, and say, "No way. Goddammit! I'm not doing that! Now, come over here and fight!" This was a risky ploy, because if they thought you were acting, they would slam you into the ropes and make you scream like a baby. You could watch their faces and read their minds. They had expected me to behave like a stoic. But a man would be a fool to make their job easy by being conventional and predictable. I could feel the tide turn in my favor at that magic moment when their anger turned to pleading: "Calm down, now calm down." The payoff would come when they decided that the risk of my going haywire in front of some touring American professor on a "fact-finding" mission was too great. More important, they had reason to believe that I would tell the truth—namely, that I had been in solitary confinement for four years and tortured fifteen times—without fear of future consequences. So theatrical training proved helpful to me.

Can you educate for leadership? I think you can, but the communists would probably say no. I think psychologists would say that leadership is innate, and there is some truth in that. But, I also think you can learn some leadership traits that naturally accrue from a good education: Compassion is a necessity for leaders, as are spontaneity, bravery, self-discipline, honesty, and above all, integrity.

I remember being disappointed about a month after I was back when one of my young friends, a prison mate, came running up after a reunion at the Naval Academy. He said with glee, "This is really great, you won't believe how this country has advanced. They've practically done away with plebe year at the Academy, and they've got computers in the basement of Bancroft Hall." I thought, "My God, if there was anything that helped us get through those eight years, it was plebe year, and if anything screwed up that war, it was computers!"

TAKING STOCK

Naval War College Review, Summer 1978

One cannot read the lectures that Alfred Thayer Mahan delivered to the War College without noting his pique at being continually challenged by his more down to earth fellow officers on the subject of his curriculum. He refers frequently and revealingly to these confrontations. For instance, during a lecture given in Luce Hall in September 1892 he remarked,

> I was in Washington a few months ago and, coming out of one of the clubs, I met on the doorstep a couple of naval officers. We stopped to talk and one asked me: "Do you expect a session of the College this year?" I replied that I hoped so. "Well," he said, "are you going to do anything practical?" I recognized my enemy at once in the noble word "practical" which had been dropped like an angel of light out of its proper sphere and significance and made to do duty against its best friends; a man's foes are often those of his own household. I endeavored to throw the burden of explanation upon my questioner. "What do you mean by practical?" I said. The reply was a little hesitating, as is apt to be the case to a categorical question and after a moment's pause he said, "Well, torpedo boats and launches and that sort of thing."

Readers may be assured that today the college has a department which addresses the employment of torpedo boats and launches and that sort of thing, as well as another which addresses Mahan's strategy and history and that sort of thing, and a third which addresses defense economics and decision-making. Since our curriculum is a matter of frequent interest to readers of our *Review*, I am using this column to announce that in addition to the core studies of the above mentioned departments, commencing this fall our students will be taking courses they select from a widely diversified extra-departmental electives program. A couple of factors prompted this change.

My own years of mid-career education changed the course of my life—it was a period of hard work to be sure, but mainly one of soul searching, of self-evaluation, of identifying those academic disciplines that encompassed what were by then well-established personal interests and affinities, of gathering in all the loose ends and aiming myself at practical service-oriented goals that made what I thought would be the best use of my talent. I had to master a battery of core subjects, of course, but also I had access to an intellectual shopping list of electives in which I could invest about a third of my time, for fun and profit. It was among those electives that I "found" myself.

Although I have intuitive feelings about educational philosophy, I did not come to the War College armed with a plan to liberalize a lock-step curriculum. As a matter of fact, what prompted my decision on the electives program was as much my perception of untapped faculty capabilities as it was my feeling that the students deserved more freedom of choice of what to study. I think it becomes obvious to anyone who strolls these halls that we have an extremely high-caliber multifaceted teaching faculty. No fixed program could hope to harness all their varied talents.

A few months ago I called this faculty together—the historians, the weapons systems engineers, the political scientists, the economists, the fleet tacticians, the systems analysts—as well as the international lawyers and the ambassador, and I said: "If you have something to say and it can be taught within the bounds of an academic discipline—that is to say, it has boundaries, it has a body of theory, it has unique assumptions, it has a literature, it has established authorities (and often a special vocabulary)—and if you can assemble a creditable reading list and lesson plans of the sort that our academic review committee would recommend as appropriate for academic credit, and further if you can draw a crowd, then I say, "Let a hundred flowers bloom, let a hundred thoughts contend."

Voluntary submissions came flowing in; the result, after all the weeding out by review committees and after my personal determination of the applicability of the course to professional military officers' education, is a slate of about 45 electives (some 17 to be offered each trimester). This fall, for instance, in addition to the core courses of the three departments, students may choose one course from among such wide-ranging subjects as "The Soviet Navy and Soviet Naval Tactics," "Advanced Electronic Warfare," "Navy Financial Management," "Applications of Operations Research," "Ocean Law and Policy," "Sino-Soviet Relations," "Constitutional Law," and so on.

This change will mean the student has considerably more control over where he wants to use his energies—20 percent worth during the year. At the same time, I want to be emphatic about the fact that for the present at least, the three department core courses will continue to demand no less than 80 percent of the student's total effort. The place where I split out from the past is in offering pertinent courses for which we have in-place faculty competence, whether within the discipline focus of the major departments or not. As I've written, when it comes to identifying fields of study that pertain to the career of a warrior, the triad of strategy, economics and operations by no means covers the waterfront; I can drive a truck through the gaps between them. Moreover, I too am a faculty member with something to say that can be taught within the bounds of an academic discipline. It may not completely surprise you that my reading list passed the test of scrutiny by the academic council or that I found the study of my favorite field (philosophy) relevant to a fighting man's responsibilities. I'll be lecturing on "Foundations of Moral Responsibility" every Wednesday and Thursday afternoon in the Mahan Library to those who choose to sign up for the course.

With this liberalization, will the dope-offs cluster around those electives in which they're already expert? I have to assume good intent, and doubt it, but if they do, so what? This is not a house of correction. Why can't a 40 year old man in the midst of a mid-career emotional and intellectual pit stop have a little time to study just what he wants? I'm reminded of some advice I got last fall from a distinguished graduate of the Naval War College, a man who for a quarter of a century has been a well-known national figure and eminent naval leader: "Jim," he said, "when you go up there, don't spend all your time trying to box in the dope-offs. The few you'll get aren't worth it, and they won't be kidding anybody. Spend your time doing your best to challenge and inspire those tigers at the other end of the spectrum. That's where the long run payoff of that institution resides."

I was honored to give the sermon below from the wineglass pulpit high above the boards in Newport's oldest (seventeenth-century) and most aristocratic church. It celebrates the independence of Rhode Island (which of course preceded the rest of the country's declaration on July 4).

INDEPENDENCE SUNDAY ⸻

Trinity Church, Newport, Rhode Island, May 7, 1978

I am always curious as I sit in a pew and watch a military man in uniform take the pulpit at one of these patriotic worship services. What is he going to say? Is he going to attempt some acrobatics of logic and come down with one foot in the camp of preparedness and the other in the camp of pacifism? Is he going to suggest that no matter what, "God is on our side"? (An argument that has always seemed to me to be at least poor sportsmanship, if not in poor taste.)

Today I'm going to play it safe—safe and smart. Safe by staying out of modern politics, referring to nothing that's been written within the last 100 years, and smart by using material that I needed to review anyway, in preparation for the philosophy course I'm going to teach this fall: "Foundations of Moral Obligation."

So, I'm going to stick to abstractions—the abstraction of human freedom. That seems appropriate. Today's *Trinity Tower* devotes its front page to it. Revolutionary Rhode Islanders lived for it. Moreover, for this church service, my material deals with Christ's conception of it.

Ex-prisoners, if you will notice, seem to be obsessed with human freedom. Many of you have probably read Viktor Frankl's book, *Man's Search for Meaning*, in which he describes his fate in a German concentration camp. He could continue resistance as long as he remembered that he, alone, was in possession of the fundamental *freedom* of shaping his own attitude about what was going on.

This morning I'm going to refer to the writings of another ex-prisoner—Fyodor Mikhailovich Dostoyevsky. A little background: Dostoyevsky was born in Moscow in 1821 of an aristocratic father and a bourgeois mother who died when he was 16. He was brought up by his father, a doctor, known to be miserly, greedy, and corrupt. The young man was educated as an engineer, entered the Czar's army as an officer, and although hardly a radical by nature had by the age of 28 gotten himself arrested, court-martialed and sentenced to death for conspiracy.

After eight months in a high-security Moscow prison he was taken into the courtyard one morning and blindfolded before a firing squad. At the last minute, in a real life drama, the Czar's messenger rode up on horseback with a reprieve. The conditions of the reprieve were rather severe. Instead of being shot he was to have four years in irons in a Siberian prison plus an additional eight years in exile from Moscow as a private soldier in a Siberian regiment. He paid his penance without bitterness. After the twelve years he returned to Moscow, became first a magazine writer, then a novelist, and now generally enjoys the reputation of being a Christian philosopher—a very Orthodox, Eastern Church Christian.

It's important that all here be aware of Dostoyevsky's legitimacy in scholarship, because the story I'm going to tell is scary and bizarre. Like many great novelists he comes across with an artful meld of overstatement, exaggeration and subtlety. It's an impressionistic story that means different things to different people—and thus I rather carefully read my remarks, and suggest that if I miss the point for you, you later read the story yourself.

What I'm talking about is really a story within a story. The book from which it comes was written when Dostoyevsky was 58, about a hundred years ago, and titled *The Brothers Karamazov. The Brothers*, as it is called in the philosophy trade, is the story of sons killing their detested father. (Perhaps Father Dostoyevsky was the model.) Don't cringe—that's not an unusual tragic theme. Sigmund Freud has classified *The Brothers* as one of the three greatest tragedies ever written, in the same league with Shakespeare's *Hamlet* and Sophocles' *Oedipus Rex*—and all three deal with parricide.

The story within the story about human freedom is told by one of the Karamozov brothers to another. It is told by the second son, Ivan, whom I would classify as a cynic, to his youngest brother, Alyosha, who like the author in his earlier days, was a novice in a monastery. (Alyosha was the name of Dostoyevsky's first son, who died at the age of three.)

Both brothers admit that the story is a fantasy. The two characters are Christ and a 90-year-old Cardinal known as the Grand Inquisitor. This fantasy took place during the Spanish Inquisition, when, so the story goes, one morning in Seville, after burning several heretics at the stake, the Cardinal noticed a crowd coming up the street and recognized the man about whom they are clustered as Christ. To get right to the point, the Cardinal, after seeing Christ perform healing miracles, decides he must be executed to save the Church.

Before you jump to conclusions, there's a couple of very important points to understand about this fantasy. First, it was Christ. It was not a case of mistaken identity and the Cardinal knew it was Christ. Second, the Cardinal was not a clerical bureaucrat or empire builder. He was too old to be ambitious to gain stature in the hierarchy of the Church, and almost too old to be vain. He is quite sympathetically portrayed as a clergyman who believed that mankind is best served, not so much by seeking the bread of heaven, as by being furnished the bread of earth—social services, and so on—of being protected from want and the ravages of war. The best way to serve man, the Cardinal might say, is to protect him from himself.

For after a lifetime of thought, and a lifetime of study of the fate of mankind in the fifteen centuries since the resurrection, the Cardinal thought that Christ had failed to take advantage of the position God had given him on earth. As he later told him, "Thou didst reject the one infallible banner which was offered Thee to make all men bow down to Thee alone." Of course, he's referring to Christ's refusal to accept the three temptations of Satan described by Matthew and Luke. He thought Christ was shortsighted and that He understood neither human nature nor the implications of Satan's three offers. I quote the Cardinal again: "In those three questions the whole subsequent history of mankind is, as it were, brought together in one whole and in them are all the unsolved contradictions of human nature." In summary, the clergyman was convinced that Christ, in his commitment to human freedom, in his insistence that man find his own ways through the earthly maze of Good and Evil, had doomed man to self-destruction.

Specifically, Christ refused to turn stones into bread and said, "Man does not live by bread alone." The Cardinal thought that by this Christ had set his standards for mankind too high, that he had foregone the opportunity to provide ample goods and services in the name of God, that he had unwittingly caused the formation of an elite group—the select who could meet his high moral standards, thereby accentuating nature's uneven distribution of human excellence—and that this in turn had spawned religious wars and so on.

The second temptation, you will remember, was Christ's refusal to demonstrate his immortality by surviving a plunge off the pinnacle. "Thou shalt not tempt the Lord thy God." By this, the Cardinal thought that Christ had passed up his chance to offer mankind that miracle, that mystery, that authority which mortals so crave. In fact, he suggests that if man does not have "miracles, mysteries and authority," he will invent them.

Throughout, with highly symbolic allusions, Dostoyevsky almost foretells the arrival of Hitler (an invented miracle), Lenin (who claimed to know what man really needed), and world federalists of various stripes—for the third temptation, as you will recall, came when Satan took Christ to a high mountain and showed him all the kingdoms of the world and said, "All these things will I give Thee if Thou will fall down and worship me."

Of course Christ refused and in the Cardinal's view thereby lost his opportunity to stop war by establishing a community of nations under his banner. For, as Dostoyevsky has his Cardinal say, "It is to mankind's advantage to live all in one unanimous, harmonious antheap of universal unity."

(The real Dostoyevsky seems to me to occasionally creep out in the prose in spite of himself.)

The Grand Inquisitor was tough. When he saw Christ raise a girl from the dead he immediately told the guards to take Him to prison. And the next day he interrogated Him (although that may be the wrong word because Christ remained silent throughout). "Why did Thee come to hinder us?" asked the Cardinal. "Fifteen centuries ago Thou said 'I will make men free' and Thou thereby imposed an intolerable burden on men, and now they lay this freedom at our priests' feet with relief." As if economic burdens were not enough, the Cardinal claimed Christ had imposed an even greater burden—a moral burden. "Nothing has brought mankind more suffering than freedom of conscience. Didst Thou forget that man prefers peace, even death, to freedom of choice in the knowledge of good and evil?" The Cardinal makes the point that humans are by nature rebellious and even criticizes God when he says, "He who created these rebellious humans must have meant to mock them." The Grand Inquisitor goes on to describe the awfulness of men left to their own devices: "They will cast down temples and drench the earth with blood."

And then enraged by Christ's silence, he continued, "Why dost Thou look silently and searchingly at me with Thy mild eyes? Be angry, I don't want Thy love for I love Thee not. And what use is it for me to hide anything from Thee? Do I not know to whom I am speaking?"

The younger Karamazov brother was incensed at such a story, as you might well be. The novice Alyosha declared: "You are merely telling me a story of a man who does not believe in God." He railed at his older brother, and asked with contempt, "How does it end?"

And Ivan replied, "When the Inquisitor ceased speaking he waited some time for his prisoner to answer him. The old man longed for Him to say something, however bitter and terrible. But suddenly Christ approached the old man in silence and softly kissed him on his bloodless, aged lips—that was all his answer. The old man shuddered, his lips moved, he went to the door, opened it and said to Christ, 'Go and come no more' and then let Him out into the dark alley of the town. The prisoner went away."

"And the old man?" asked Alyosha. Ivan replied, "The kiss glows in his heart, but the old man adheres to his idea."

Rather an odd story, such as ex-prisoners are wont to tell on occasion. And like the stories of T. E. Lawrence (*Seven Pillars of Wisdom*), and of several of us other ex-prisoners, it is subject to interpretation. I've already tipped my hand on how I interpret this one, as I presumed Dostoyevsky tipped his hand with his use of the word "antheap." Another telltale word is "clever," because at least twice the Cardinal refers to himself as one who has forsaken Christ and joined the other, "more clever" people. In one of his last punch lines the Grand Inquisitor admonishes Christ by saying: "Thou didst lift men up and taught them to be proud. We, however, shall show them that they are weak and that they are only children. But we'll explain how we will make them happy and that childlike happiness is sweetest of all."

Today, we celebrate the memory of some Rhode Islanders who 202 years ago certainly did not come down on the side of the "childlike happiness" of serving even a benevolent master. They were free, self-determining souls in the true sense of the word—proud, brave, passionate, some cruel, some acquisitive, many generous, almost all conscience-ridden (as only Protestant New Englanders can be), and all obsessed with independence and freedom—bearing all those burdens of which the Grand Inquisitor would have relieved them. Rhode Islanders above all other ex-colonials were scarcely shy of accepting the obligation of seeking their own resolution of the problems of good and evil. Each was dedicated to finding his own way to God. And they knew there was a price for that pride and that freedom and that independence—and periodically it has been paid in blood. But who wants to live in an antheap?

In early May of 1776 Rhode Island declared for liberty. Fourteen years later in May of 1790 they committed themselves to the common pursuit of liberty with the other twelve colonies by signing a Constitution whose preamble states as its purpose, "To establish justice, to ensure domestic tranquility, to provide for the common defense, and to promote the general welfare." And I am one who believes that the order in which our Founding Fathers chose to list those purposes, that is, justice first, domestic tranquility second, defense third, and welfare fourth, was intentional.

A commencement address is an opportunity for a special kind of teaching; I always enjoy the occasion.

WHAT YOU WILL BE _____

Commencement Address, Salve Regina College, Newport, Rhode Island, May 21, 1978

Graduation means different things to different people. For most it casts mixed feelings of sweetness and dismay—the sweetness from knowing that for the next few hours at least, one is not going to have that feeling of being behind on a paper or project, and the dismay from the vacuum—the melancholy that seems to creep into one's consciousness as he comes to realize full that a hard-fought battle is over, and that he has won. I refer to that "bitterness of an end achieved" of which Somerset Maugham writes in his short story, "Mayhew." Another sad aspect of graduation is saying goodbye to people, to your fellow students with whom you have been associated and with whom you hopefully have established a good reputation. And now you must go out and reestablish that reputation all over again with faces yet unseen. A third common feeling is the onset of anxiety about the niche you will make for yourself in life. I am not talking about paying the grocery bill; I am talking about thoughts of what you're going to become—what you will be, as opposed to what you will have. My purpose this morning is to ease the anxiety that might accompany that third natural feeling at graduation.

Late last night I left Washington, D.C., where I have been closeted since

Tuesday with eleven Rear Admirals as President of the selection board appointed to pick our 1979 crop of new Navy Captains. I will leave again this afternoon to continue that process. Being a part of such an important selection is an emotional workout, an education, and a revelation. It is natural to wax philosophical as you see men's lifetime records portrayed on screens, as you and your board of experienced officers go over these records in the traditional, methodical, and (I am quick to say) fair way to judge not who deserves reward, but who shows the most promise for seasoned and productive leadership in the years ahead; that is to say, in their late 40s and 50s. The people in contention before this board are all well beyond the age of being remembered largely for their collegiate efforts. They are far enough along in life to be justly held accountable for the output of enterprises that they themselves initiated; accountable not only for the way they behaved but for the way men they molded behaved. They are no longer men of just the theoretical world but men of the practical world. They now know what that old intellectual, Professor Hans Morgenthau, meant when he said

> . . . in the world of the intellectual, ideas meet with ideas, and anything goes that is presented cleverly and with assurance. But in the practical world, ideas meet with facts, facts which make mincement of wrong ideas and throw the pieces in the ashcan of history.

I've said that my purpose in making these remarks is to allay anxiety. I can't think of anything that would give today's graduate of Salve Regina more feeling of self-confidence than to be a fly on the wall at a mid-career promotion selection deliberation, civilian or military, to see for himself how heavily humans standing in judgment, particularly those judging where best to place special trust and confidence, rely on the homely virtues and eschew the frills. On the basis of last week's contemplation I would like to identify four traits that seem to me common among those who are assured a place in history.

The first is that of being predisposed to continual self-improvement. Those who have it are dynamically regenerative, they gain momentum as they go along and don't rest on their laurels. People who have this trait seldom make the same mistake twice; the pattern of self-improvement is clear in their records. Shortcomings are followed by self-imposed remedial study. Men once criticized for poor speaking or writing are praised for excellence in these same skills five years later. In my mind, the prototype of these thinking, self-propelled people is the man who escorted me here to the lectern—a man who perceived the impact of the nuclear age ahead of his peers, and went out on his own time and with his own resources got his Ph.D. in the applicable sciences, long before Service sponsorship of such education became institutionalized. I am talking about your school's Trustee and Executive Board member, Admiral Chick Hayward. He and those like him are creative men with clarity of thought and energy of will (which is almost a definition of genius) capable of effective responses to new situations (which is a definition of intelligence). They bring much from their undergraduate experience but none of it so important as their self-discipline. Self-discipline can come from college, too. As John Ruskin said 150 years ago, "Education does not mean teaching people what they do not know, it means teaching them to behave as they do not behave."

A second trait, and one I don't think I need to spend much time on because I think you are familiar with how I feel about it, is integrity. To urge you all to have it is not a statement of piety but practical advice. Anyone who has lived in an extortion environment (and we've all lived in one of one sort or another) realizes that the potential weapon of the adversary before which all his other threats fall is his manipulation of his victim's shame. A clear conscience is one's only protection. The surest way to wind up in the ashcan of history is to have a reputation of indirectness or deceit. There is something in all of us who stand in judgment, when we are down to the wire and the choices are limited, to prefer to work with loyal, steadfast plodders rather than devious geniuses.

A third trait of people destined to be successful is that of having the emotional stability to handle failure. The inculcation of that quality is the great challenge of education; few people have to be taught to handle success. The only way I know to learn to handle failure is to gain historic perspective and to be familiar with examples of men who have successfully coped with failure in the classical and religious past. I am reminded of the old quotation of the philosopher of the Book of Ecclesiastes who was so well regarded by us in prison and who so correctly anticipated our reaction to the fate of many of our old friends at home during our prolonged absence:

> I returned and saw that the race is not always to the swift nor the battle to the strong, neither yet bread to the wise nor riches to men of understanding, nor favors to men of skill, but time and chance happeneth to them all.

Realizing that that is the way of the world is a very important part of education.

The fourth attribute, of course, is that of leadership ability. I think the sort of military leadership that takes San Juan Hill is an indispensable trait in my profession. But today I speak of another, broader version of leadership; a quality which can properly be called *teachership*. That is to say, to have the ability to set the moral, social, and particularly the motivational tone among those with whom you work. This takes wisdom; you have to have the sensitivity to perceive philosophic disarray in your charges. I use the term charges because teachership or education involves not only wielding authority but practicing stewardship. Great achievers are usually those who take the pains to relate the enterprise being addressed to its practical societal worth and to the cultural heritage of its architects. This is a very formidable challenge and one for which you cannot get too much education. As I look back over my life, in and out of the Service, the great leaders I've met have in reality been teachers of great understanding, patience, compassion, and courage. Leadership or teachership, as the same John Ruskin says, "is a painful, continual and difficult work to be done by kindness, by waiting, by warning, by precept, by praise, but above all by example."

I bring forth my observations on the universality of these four traits among the successful because they are relevant to this Class of '78. They are not only military attributes. In fact, self-discipline, integrity, historical perspective and sensitivity to cultural heritage and societal worth are the stated educational goals in the Salve Regina catalog. And what better place to acquire them than here in a school that devotes itself to teaching the liberal arts, the arts which at their bases are: reading, writing, speaking, listening, figuring—the indispensable arts that always apply no matter what's going on in the world. Moreover, be thankful that you learned these arts in a Christian college as a part of the greater process of transmitting from generation to generation the creative principle, the traditions and the religious and classical culture of the Western world.

This is a process that hopefully will have made you forever conscious of a history that makes us what we are: products of the culture of Greece, inherited by the Romans and transferred by the Fathers of the Church with the religious teaching of Christianity and progressively enlarged by a countless number of artists, writers, scientists and philosophers from the beginning of the Middle Ages until now. I also hope this education will make you forever conscious of *who* we are: mortals who have learned to regard ourselves as inviolable persons because we are rational and free. We are capable of comprehending the moral order of the universe and our place in that order, performing duties it imposes upon us and exercising the rights that it bestows.

Be thankful you have studied in an institution that has not deprived you of learning of your cultural heritage. Believe it or not, you have gained a distinction held by very few people nowadays. As a result you may be among the few who will someday be able to keep this civilization glued together; for as the sanity of an individual is dependent upon the continuity of his memories, so also is the sanity of a civilization dependent upon the continuity of its traditions. You, through one chance or another, may come to see face to face as I have the fragility of the thin veneer of civilization that coats a world of barbarism. Strong and confident men, normally supported by the conventions and props of a familiar culture can be reduced to insecure and sobbing animals in a matter of days or even hours when alone and in misery.

I can remember a Sunday morning in Hanoi when a new wailing and crying voice could be heard from a cell in a far corner of the prison. One of my friends established contact and found a great hulk of an American—a college athlete—reduced through the pain of unattended broken limbs, through prolonged thirst, through the confusion of five days on the road with mean and non-communicative handlers, and through humiliation (his trousers caked with filth) to a crazed and delirious state. The American voice that spoke to him calmed him, and in a day's time, in spite of his pain and deprivation, he returned to being the confident, mature fellow he was before and is today. Thus it is when a good man is forced off this narrow ledge of civilization.

The thin veneer of civilization that we know is precious. It is also modern. We could seat in this room, this auditorium, a couple, man and wife, representing each generation of man since he acquired his present appearance and characteristics, about 50,000 years ago. There would be only about 800 couples. But stop and think; to us most of them would seem quite odd. The first 650 of the couples would have lived in caves, only the last 70 would have had effective means of communicating with their fellow man, and only the last 6 would have ever seen a printed page.

Our culture, our link with sanity, our shield against barbarism is fragile. With the diploma issued by this college that has so encouraged an understanding and appreciation of it, I charge you with our culture's care and protection. It has been said that "somebody has to guard the passes." And why not you who have thankfully learned the value of what you are protecting?

And along with this responsibility I ask you to remember that you have here acquired the keys to great achievement. You have been given the historical perspective to cope with failure and rise again another day, the sensitivity to teach and inspire, the discipline necessary for self-correction, and, the Lord willing, a character in which integrity thrives. May you use these attributes well. Good luck and Godspeed.

TAKING STOCK

Naval War College Review, Fall 1978

Press reaction to Aleksandr Solzhenitsyn's Harvard address last spring was extraordinary. Editorial comment was voluminous, frequently registered surprise at what one would assume were his well-known viewpoints, and seemed to avoid his major thrusts. In particular, most writers missed or ignored his principal premise, one common to almost all the Solzhenitsyn titles which have lined American library shelves for the past fifteen years, and one with which I agree. While not wanting to use the *Naval War College Review* as a forum for debating whether Solzhenitsyn is on target or not, I believe his concept of the insidiousness of creeping legalism is relevant to our fighting forces and bears investigation. The mutation of ethics in a legalistic society is a very thought-provoking subject and it strikes me as odd that the editorial writers of this country bypassed it. For me, the problem boils down to displacement of personal responsibility by law in what has become an essentially litigious society, where moral goodness is defined as conformity to specified rules of conduct and where personal virtue or righteousness is considered synonymous with a mechanical disposition to submit consistently to those rules.

The flagrant, excessive use of laws, courts, regulations and the growing penchant for directing society's course by a myriad of rules has largely and sadly depreciated the worth of assuming moral responsibility. No longer are individuals expected to make determinations of right or wrong. Now they can justify nearly every action by some rule, some technicality, either written or conceived, for the appeals process. The product of this letter of the law society is measured on the legal-versus-illegal scale with the good-versus-bad scale only rarely being applied, more often than not as a matter of convenience. Society as a whole has adopted the judicial process as its moral yardstick and forfeited common sense and personal responsibility. Legal is not necessarily synonymous with good.

This situation exists to a great extent in the U.S. military profession in which too many officers are armed only with technical knowledge and a legalistic, by-the-numbers approach; this type of person proceeds through his career tripping over minutiae and substituting checkoff lists for common sense. Too many have become relativists without any defined moral orientation. Too many are content to align their value systems with fads and buzzwords, and mindlessly try to obey what amounts to a hodgepodge mixture of inconsistent slogans. Error avoidance and careerism are seen to take the place of positive achievement within our ranks.

What is to be done? If one looks at the West's cultural heritage, particularly at its roots in the classical writings, there seem to be several important guideposts designed to discourage what Solzhenitsyn calls a "letter of the law" mentality that "paralyzes men's noblest impulses." Aristotle frequently distinguished between the ethics of character and the ethics of acts by suggesting that society's main objective is to instill virtue in its citizenry, and that specific laws are a secondary concern. In fact, most philosophers of the classical Greek rationalistic tradition treated dispositions of character as primary and specific rules of conduct as secondary and derivative. We must realize that laws merely delineate a floor in our behavior, a minimum acceptable level of ethical standards, and that moral standards can and should be set on a higher plane. In the Naval Service we have no place for amoral gnomes lost in narrow orbits; we need to keep our gaze fixed on the high-minded principles standing above the law: Duty, Honor, Country.

A meaning to life can only be gained through an intuitive sense of good and bad and their attendant comparatives (worse, worst, better, best). It does not obtain directly from systems of laws emanating either from the legislative or the judiciary sides, and can be positively strangled by the real culprit in our national investment in moral bankruptcy—the delegation of lawmaking powers to the administrative bodies who work far from the canons of ethics and decency. Such social regulation is the disease that Solzhenitsyn diagnoses as totally lacking an ethical base.

It is certainly convenient to adopt the mores of the bureaucracy and not take on the unpleasant and tedious task of formulating one's own. However, if anything has power to sustain an individual in peace or war, regardless of occupation, it is one's conviction and commitment to define standards of right and wrong. Today's ranks are filled with officers who have been weaned on slogans and fads of the sort preached in the better business schools of the country. That is to say that rational managerial concepts will cure all evils. The flaws of this viewpoint are brightly illuminated when it is applied to fighting forces—that's one of the things Vietnam proved. The loss of that war demonstrated that we cannot adopt the methodology of business without adopting its language, its style, its tactics, and above all, its ethics. We must regain our bearings.

It is time to put the legal machinery in its proper place: to aid the people in maintaining order and seeking truth. However, regardless of the fairness of our judicial system it must not be allowed to take the place of moral obligation to ourselves, to our service, to our country. Each man must bring himself to some stage of ethical resolution. I hope this message will travel far beyond the walls of Mahan Hall where I will be expounding it this year.

THE USS *BELLEAU WOOD*

Commissioning Ceremony, Pascagoula, Mississippi, September 23, 1978

We are gathered today to celebrate the commissioning of a naval combatant of rare dimension. I approach this podium with a deep respect and pride for what our countrymen have accomplished in this beautiful ship's design and construction and for what her gallant crew will accomplish for our nation in the future. Today the word "prospective" disappears from all ship's company titles, and the many deeds done since the keel was laid will suddenly become history. This ship will proceed to join the amphibious forces of our Pacific Fleet and will provide an essential lift capability to land Marines anywhere along the rim of that biggest of all oceans. This ship provides the means to move a landing force rapidly to an objective and to get those Marines ashore quickly.

As the third ship of this class, *Belleau Wood* supports our ability to contain crises or to directly intervene. Deployment of amphibious forces has always struck a sensitive chord in the hearts of our adversaries. It signals commitment and the arrival of Marines who will stay. Having lived in a country under siege for nearly eight years, I can tell you firsthand of the anxiety which an impending amphibious landing holds for the enemy. Nothing gets their attention faster than threats or rumors of Marines coming ashore. Enemy problems, which under the press of experience and accommodation have a way over years of prolonged war of becoming almost hypothetical, suddenly become very real.

This ship is made up of two parts: the hardware and the men. It is 800 plus feet of the highest technology, the best American shipbuilding provides; the second largest type ship of our Navy line, she will form a nucleus of our amphibious forces into the 21st century. *Belleau Wood* combines the missions of four ships. She provides a dual thrust—a troop and materiel quick transport capability which can have 1000 marines on the beach in eight minutes, moving by helicopter and landing craft.

And thank God she can. On the way down here I read the recent Christopher Buckley article in the latest *Esquire* magazine which describes the Soviet Union's serious entry into the amphibious warfare world with their ROGOV class ships. These new fifteen thousand ton vessels can disgorge a naval infantry battalion, with tanks, quickly from boats, from a well deck, from helicopters, and from air cushion vehicles. Of course, *Belleau Wood* is bigger, fast, capable, versatile and has that tenacity of greater staying power. Yet technology and hardware are only half the vessel. As my old friend, Anthony Sokol—ex-naval officer and octogenarian scholar of war from Stanford University—has written, "The principles taught by history are as valuable in these days of automation as at any other time; and it is clear that the human element is the decisive factor in war as well as in peace, and that man's ingenuity, courage, and determination can overcome seemingly insurmountable obstacles and achieve the apparently impossible."

Ladies and gentlemen, the crew you see before you is well-trained, professional, dedicated and proud. This is a unique team, ready to go in harm's way if called.

Over the past 30 years, on more than 200 occasions six Presidents have elected to deploy a military presence. Our Navy was the instrument used in over 80% of those occasions. Although the ship has been designed from the keel up for its amphibious mission, she can also be employed in situations short of war to warn potential aggressors of our stand should his provocations continue. *Belleau Wood*'s flexibility and punching power offer the credibility that spells deterrence in a world marred by violence. And it's not likely that this world's propensity for violence will change: in only a few hundred of the thousands of years of recorded history has this planet been free of the blight of ongoing war. So we must be prepared.

Although *Belleau Wood* was actually born at its keel-laying and took form with its christening, this commissioning ceremony marks its first life's breath. On this day, one feels the exhilaration which accompanies something hoped for, the fulfillment of men's dreams, and their labors. Today *Belleau Wood* becomes a living thing, with a unique and colorful heritage rooted in two world wars.

I remember going aboard the first USS *Belleau Wood* during my plebe summer of 1943 at the Naval Academy. Just commissioned, she had been laid down as a new cruiser, a USS *New Haven*, but was one of several of that class equipped with a flat top and commissioned as a CVL to meet the pressing need for carrier air in the Pacific. Active throughout the atoll campaigns, and later off Japan, her action reports recount almost daily combat between the embarked air group and the enemy. She was cited for destroying a Japanese aircraft carrier singlehanded. And, I'm sorry to say, 92 men of her crew were later killed by a kamikaze plane that crashed on her flight deck.

The postwar statistics are impressive. After four years in commission, *Belleau Wood* had logged over 200,000 miles, accounting for the destruction of over 500 enemy aircraft, sinking 12 heavy and 36 light ships and inflicting damage on 83 others. She was awarded a Presidential Unit Citation for "Extraordinary heroism against Japanese forces in the air, ashore, and afloat." She won 12 Battle Stars. Transferred to France in 1953, she served their navy for six years under her French name *Bois-Belleau*. In 1960 she returned to Boston and was sold for scrap. Such is the life and death of a capital ship.

As you have all read in your program, a little further back in history is the battle for which both these USS *Belleau Wood*s have been named. Some historians call it the turning point of World War I. Many describe it as the battle that saved Paris. All agree it was crucial. Moreover, it was a battle in which the United States Marine Corps gained its modern identity as the elite of the world's elite fighting units.

The Belleau Wood was an hourglass-shaped picnic area which occupied about a third of a 640 acre section of land, only 80 kilometers from Paris. It was the size of a small family farm, located not quite as far from Paris' Eiffel Tower as this pier is from Mobile. That's where the 4th Marines stopped a hand-picked corps of the Kaiser's army on its final thrust to Paris and victory. As the first U.S. Marine captain marched into the wood, he was met by a French army major leading his beaten, exhausted soldiers away from the front, away from the bombardment of those crack German troops. The French major said the order of march was to the rear. As your program tells you, the marine ignored the order and said, "Retreat, hell, we just got here."

Soon thereafter, in that normally pastoral wood, erupted some of the bloodiest fighting of World War I—much of it hand-to-hand. After stopping the German thrust, troops of the 5th and 6th Marine Regiments launched a devastating counteroffensive. More than half our 9000 man Marine Brigade became casualties before it was all over. This was the battle which earned the Corps that coveted legacy of "holding the line" when men of lesser commitment would say retreat.

General Black Jack Pershing gave his Chief of Staff command of the Marine Brigade with the warning, "I'm giving you the best Brigade in France. If anything goes wrong, I'll know who is to blame." This was the battle that endeared the Corps to America, as reporter Floyd Gibbons' stories were spread across the front pages of every newspaper. It was a battle which brought a new vocabulary to men's lips—with "cooties" our Marines' name for French body lice—with "foxholes"—their name for shallow dugouts— and a name of German origin for our Marines themselves, which they in turn accepted with pride, the "Devil Dogs."

It was a battle that produced national heroes at an amazing rate. Sgt. Dan Daly, a 45-year-old gunnery sergeant, a double Medal of Honor winner for action at Peking in 1900 and at Haiti in 1915, embodied the spirit of those Marines. At one point Daly stood up in a hail of fire and urged his men forward against the enemy with the cry, "What's the matter with you sons o' bitches, do you want to live forever?"

It was a battle which made the survivors a combat-seasoned force which has never been equaled. Four future USMC Commandants fought there during those three weeks. Belleau Wood was a costly piece of real estate. But the German advance had been stopped, setting the stage for the Allies' successful conclusion of the war.

Belleau Wood will always be a watchword of our sea services. In particular, they've given you *Belleau Wood* sailors and Marines something to remember—something to be proud of.

So, as I look over this flight deck, I feel that although this ship is new, in a sense it is very old. I hope that those present on this very special day will pause to think about their history and acknowledge their heritage. *Belleau Wood* is not merely a product of the shipwright's skills; she is a living legend, a dynamic memorial whose own history begins today. My experience has shown that under pressure a sense of history is what holds us together. And this ship is an institution.

In my mind's eye I can see the Sgt. Dan Dalys of tomorrow standing on this flight deck, looking toward the beach, prepared for a war we all hope will never come. Thank you.

TAKING STOCK ────────────

Naval War College Review, Winter 1979

Practical men tell us it's a good idea from time to time to check our assets against our liabilities. Today we are long on technical knowledge, short on courage. For light on hard topics like courage I like to start with a ray of ancient wisdom.

Aristotle was a practical hardnosed scholar and no-nonsense teacher. He wrote the first textbooks for a dozen academic disciplines including physics, biology, logic, psychology and political science. Although time has passed him by in some fields, a recent winner of a Nobel prize for genetic research said that the award should rightly go to the old master from whose treatise on embryology he lifted some of his prize-winning ideas on sperm chemistry. Skeptics may chuckle about that, but in the area of moral philosophy, Aristotle's preeminence endures. In the field of military ethics, Aristotle is one of the few writers who actually spells out the qualities that one rightly expects to find in the heart of a warrior, whether a fighting man of the 5th century B.C. or of World War III.

The exemplary moral virtue of a military man, says Aristotle, is courage. Because it is a moral virtue, involving feeling as well as reason, one achieves it by avoiding the pitfalls of excess (rashness) or defect (cowardice). In this way Aristotle introduces his concept of moral excellence—the mean. The mean doesn't signify "moderate" or fencesitting, but rather the center of a target, avoiding on the one hand gutlessness and on the other show-off irresponsibility. Endurance is a major component of the classical Greek concept of courage. Aristotle's teacher, Plato, defined courage as "endurance of the soul." Although the Greeks acknowledge the value of the single brave thrust or audacious dash, their hero was more often the man who "hung in there" when the going got tough. Both Plato and Aristotle specified that courage had to be exercised in the presence of fear. Aristotle described courage as the measure of man's ability to handle fear.

A correlative of courage is the ability to deal with failure. Just as a military leader is expected to handle fear with courage, so also should we expect him to handle failure with emotional stability—another way of saying endurance of soul. I'm not talking about the leader being a "good loser"; I mean his ability to meet personal defeat with neither the defect of emotional paralysis and withdrawal nor the excess of lashing out at scapegoats or inventing escapist solutions. (Faced with monstrous ingratitude from his children, King Lear found solace in insanity. The German people, swamped with merciless economic hardships, sought solace in Adolf Hitler.)

Humans seem to have an inborn need to believe that in this universe a natural moral economy prevails by which evil is punished and virtue is rewarded. When it dawns on trusting souls that no such moral economy is operative in this life some of them come unglued. Aristotle had a name for the Greek drama about "good men with a flaw who come to unjustified bad ends"—tragedy. The control of tragedy in this sense is the job of education. The only way I know how to handle failure is to gain historical perspective, to think about men who have successfully lived with failure in our religious and classical past. When we were in prison we remembered the Book of Ecclesiastes: "I returned and saw that the race is not always to the swift nor the battle to the strong, neither yet bread to the wise nor riches to men of understanding, nor favors to men of skill, but time and chance happeneth to them all."

Today the statement that life is not fair has drawn ridicule. But it's true nevertheless. For that interpretation of a good man's defeat I prefer the original poem of the Book of Job—the way it was before some ancient revisionist historian spliced on a happy ending. The story of Job goes a long way in explaining the "Why me?" of failure. That God can allow evil to be visited upon upright and honest men is something we must be prepared to deal with.

How does one handle failure? One can develop or learn that special kind of courage that can prepare us for the occurrence of failure and diminish its worst effects. Historical perspective allows us to assess within the framework of the past the relative importance of injury and disappointment—even a misfortune that may seem cataclysmic and the end of the world. Measured historical perspective will allow an optimism of hard work to grow. That's my definition for a studied outlook born of knowing that failure is not the end of everything, that a man can always pick himself up off the canvas and fight one more round.

TAKING STOCK ⸻

Naval War College Review, February 1979

In my frantic rush to catch up on the eight years of American history that I missed, I am often appalled by the studied, analytic approach to warfare taken by so many of the educated, well-intentioned individuals who directed our war in Vietnam. If my understanding of their reasoning is to remain lacking, so much the better. For he who supports the position that warfare and warriors are just other things to which the rational concepts of business and economics apply, is missing the mark. Lewis Sorley reviews *Crisis in Command* in the Professional Reading section of this *Review* and I think his opening assessment of the book is accurate: the book is flawed. Gabriel and Savage's little volume has been condemned by many as an exaggerated indictment of American performance in Vietnam; many say it is hung on a questionable historic framework, and almost all its readers agree that its suggested reforms are reminiscent of the Dark Ages. Though acknowledging all of that, Sorley again hits the nail on the head when he adds: to dismiss this book for the above reasons, however, is to ignore the tremendous power of the authors' central thesis. That thesis is that American victory was impossible because our traditional fighting man's gladiatorial ethic had been programmed out of style and supplanted by an entrepreneurial ethic whose tools were based on the rational corporate model, systems analysis and utils. This new fad assumed that management and leadership were synonymous. Natural outgrowths of that concept were officers' ticket punching, organizational efficiency at the expense of honor, and ultimately a breakdown of small fighting unit cohesion, spirit and integrity.

Wars cannot be fought the same way bureaucrats haggle over apportionments. The toll of human life in battle does not lend itself to cost/benefit analysis. One's plan of action on the international chessboard cannot be built on compromise businesslike decisions among factions. To design a country's strategy along a middle course for bureaucratic reasons is to aim at what Winston Churchill has called the bull's-eye of disaster. That our country was steady on course for that bull's-eye of disaster, even before I was shot down in September 1965, is evident from a reading of Admiral U.S. Grant Sharp's recent book *Strategy for Defeat*. By that time, the bureaucracy was already sending him, CINCPAC, waffled directives (consensus documents with "all factions inside the paper") that were not consistent with the stated military objectives of that same bureaucracy. The managerial authors of the war policy spoke self-assuredly in the language of war but their mind-set continued to be that of faddish entrepreneurial gamesmen; by the time they realized that the enemy was ignoring their finesses, it had long been clear to those in the field that these gamesmen had no belly for a fight. With forces already committed, there was no place to go but down.

The style, ethics and language of business are peculiar to that vocation. So too does war have its own style, ethics and language. Clausewitz wrote: "War is a special profession, however general its relation may be and even if all the male population of a country capable of bearing arms were able to practice it, war would still continue to be different and separate from any other activity which occupies the life of man." Contrast this with a paragraph from a study done in 1974 entitled *U.S. Tactical Air Power*: "Waging war is no different in principle from any other resource transformation process and should be just as eligible for the improvements in proficiency that have accrued elsewhere from technological substitution." This is simply not true. There are men who in battle can realize proficiency that would be labeled "impossible" by any systems analyst, men who can make $2+2=5$ time after time on the basis of their personal courage, leadership, strength, loyalty, and comradeship. When the chips are down, and you're facing real uncertainty instead of that on a projected Profit and Loss sheet, you need something more than rationalist stuffing. The first step is to acknowledge that fighting men resent being manipulated by carrot and stick enticements; they find no solace in being part of some systematic resource transformation process when they're told to go in harm's way. In short, you can't program men to their deaths; they have to be led, and, as *Crisis in Command* points out, high risks and high casualty rates for senior officers are common elements of victory.

Thus, though I take issue with some of the assertions in *Crisis in Command*, I think it carries a strong message for leadership. Whether we're driving ships around the ocean or navigating a desk ashore, all of us in the military should continually contemplate that "different and separate activity which occupies the life of man." As we follow the peacetime horde down the prescribed track, let us not adopt the false sense of security that combat philosophies will be issued by "the system" when the need arises. The twists and turns of the fortunes of war have a way of throwing military men into new decision-making territory where all previous bets are off and no philosophic survival kits are available. Have you thought it through? When the whistle blows, are you ready to step out of your business suit with both the philosophy and the belly for a fight?

TAKING STOCK

Naval War College Review, March–April 1979

After nearly two academic years at the helm of this institution, I can appreciate the thoughtful and studied progress of its 95-year history and can understand the changes in style, curriculum and focus that have evolved over time to support the original goal of studying the profession of arms. That goal remains our raison d'être and hasn't changed since General Order No. 325 was issued in 1884. As we shape our curriculum and procedures for the Class of 1980, I'd like to take the opportunity to review the bidding and to express some of the educational philosophy that underlies the changes I've made and determines the direction we're going.

Educating people to make sound decisions has never been a simple process, nor is designing the curriculum to do it. A realistic program of study must be uniformly rigorous yet encourage original thinking. It must include a survey of what's new in technology, tactics and foreign affairs as well as foundation work in the immutable lessons of history. Four principal activities comprise our curriculum: the traditional prescribed courses in Strategy and Policy, Defense Economics, Naval Operations and the Electives program. The three prescribed courses are offered at both the senior and intermediate levels with a distinct variation in focus that reflects prospective needs of future assignments.

We've made a conscious shift to war gaming in the Naval Operations course, and our students participate to an ever increasing extent in major CINC-level games during the year. With the completion of our new facility in 1980, I see the trend continuing towards more and more gaming activity at all levels. The reputation of the Naval War College was built largely on the tremendous impact gaming had on World War II. As Nimitz later wrote, "The enemy of our games was always—Japan—and the courses were so thorough that after the start of World War II—nothing that happened in the Pacific was strange or unexpected."

The Electives program has been a most enlightening educational experiment and for the Class of 1980 it will have equal status and credit weight with the prescribed courses. About 90 percent of our students are able to get their first choice of an array of sixteen electives each trimester. The selections thus far have revealed a marked interest in area studies (Russia, China, Middle East), Electronic Warfare and Soviet studies. I am of course delighted with the response to my "Foundations of Moral Obligation" which I team teach with Dr. Joseph Brennan, professor emeritus of philosophy at Columbia University. We will offer that twice again next year. Additionally, the Naval War College will be privileged next spring trimester to have in residence Dr. Philip Rhinelander, professor emeritus of philosophy at Stanford University where he was also Dean. My old friend Philip has additionally been director of general education at Harvard, and a Boston lawyer before that. He is now teaching philosophy of law at Stanford while writing a new book on law and morality that will be the text for a special elective course entitled "The Scope and Function of Morality" for the NWC Class of 1980.

Philosophy is the logical discipline from which to draw insights and inspirations into military leadership in general, and combat virtues in particular. In my view, trendy psychological chitchat case study leadership courses usually wind up in a welter of relativism. In fact, current literature tells me that the social sciences as a whole are becoming committed to a veritable ideology of relativism, an "egalitarianism of ideas" via the route of a logical positivism that most philosophers have long since rejected. If one leads men into battle while committed to the idea that each empirically unverifiable value judgment is just as good as the next, he's in for trouble. Thus, I think offerings of a discipline whose founder (Socrates) was committed to the position that there is such a thing as central, objective truth, and that that which is *just* transcends self-interest, provide a sensible contrast to much of today's management and leadership literature.

A quality program is thus in store for this first class of the new decade, in each of the four parts of our curriculum. Throughout its preparation we in Newport will be guided by a historic precedent that has consistently emphasized process over perishable content, concentration over fragmentation and education over training. We will continue to require that students read widely and critically, write extensively and analytically and define their ideas forcefully and logically in graduate-level seminars.

The quality of the academic excellence of any institution is tied directly to the rigor of its curriculum. Grades are an important and necessary adjunct to this rigor. For the Class of 1980, I have made a departure from the traditional 4.0 grading system and have implemented a straightforward A, B, C format. However, grades will be considered privileged information, and they will not appear in any fitness or efficiency reports. In fact, they will be released from the college only on the request of the student who earned them; this is an important provision, particularly because Naval War College transcripts have become increasingly valuable for accreditation and admission to other institutions. (Each year our Registrar processes 150 transcript requests from our graduates.) To summarize my position on grades for the Class of 1980, I am continuing to assume that they are an important form of communication between professor and student in our education processes. But I do not want the process of grading to generate a rat race or result in a senseless competition that inhibits a mature officer's desire to concentrate study time on issues in which his interest is piqued. Subordination of our educational goals to the relentless logic of a measurement system based on weighted coefficients is not what is desired here. The provisions herein are designed to free all from any shackles, save their desire to learn and thereby better serve their country.

I hope this "academic report" gives the alumni, friends, and particulary the inbound Class of 1980 a clear picture of what we're doing in Newport. I think of the academic year as an intellectual and philosophical "pit stop" that should give military officers a fresh, positive frame of mind as they glance down the track at the second half of their careers. This is where the creativity and measured outlook gained (I hope) during their War College experience realize utility. We try to build the self-confidence our students will need to fashion that most important and productive part of their careers around their individual strengths. So, Class of 1980, we see our job as one of boosting you to a tall ship and hope that in the process we may help you find a star to steer her by.

CURRENT STRATEGY AND RUSSIAN NAVAL POWER

Opening Remarks, Annual Current Strategy Forum, Naval War College, Newport, Rhode Island, May 3, 1979

Before I introduce our Chief of Naval Operations, I want to take just a few minutes as President of this institution to welcome you three hundred guests to this annual forum. It's a pleasure to have you. You represent different backgrounds, different interests, different professions, different disciplines, and of course, different convictions, but we are Americans all and all here to consider how this Republic fares vis-à-vis the Soviet Union.

A few words to those of you who are not familiar with our Naval War College and what goes on here: This is one of what I call the triad of major educational institutions of the U.S. Navy. This triad consists of the Naval Academy founded in 1845, the Naval Postgraduate School started in 1911, and this War College which dates back to 1884. The first President of this institution was Stephen B. Luce. It was the first Senior Service college in America and is now the oldest war college in the world. The three institutions of our Navy's triad are unique among American military schools in that all three rely largely on civilian faculties for continuity and academic rigor. The faculties of each are in fact half civilian and half military. We are very proud of our faculty here in Newport. We have about 30 civilian Ph.D.s in the disciplines of history, political science, economics, psychology and systems analysis from the best universities in the country, and they team up with a like number of seasoned captains and colonels who also have advanced degrees. The main student body consists of 400 Americans, half of whom are about 35 years old (the so-called junior class); the other half are about age 42, the senior class or, as we say, the College of Naval Warfare. Of the 400, approximately half are naval officers, the rest from other Services and civilian governmental agencies. There are also two groups of foreign officers here under instruction: the Naval Command College consists of 40 captains from allied navies, no two of whom are from the same country; we also have a junior course of foreign officers in the lieutenant commander rank bracket.

Our academic year is ten and a half months long. The curriculum has four parts: one of the mandatory subjects is Strategy and Policy, which is actually a case study of history; this highlights the various uses of military power since fifth century Athens. Another core discipline is what we call Defense Economics, sometimes known as Management, and a third is, of course, Naval Operations, which is the study of naval tactics as applied to our fleets. The latter subject is practiced and studied at our big war-gaming center which is down the street about half a block. The fourth part of the curriculum consists of elective studies; all of our faculty expertise is utilized in subjects ranging from financial management to electronic warfare to moral philosophy.

This diversified and yet rather conventional array of academic offerings, the faculty and the student body, make up this Naval War College which you visit today. The faint-hearted have tried to take the word war out of our school's title from time to time, but I would never stand for it because war is what we study here. And why should humans not study it? It is part of the human predicament and I think that all who come here, including you and me, are committed to the view that it is better to study this predicament than to put your head in the sand and consider it a temporary aberration in the life of man. This week we will be dealing with war—dealing with power—national power. One of my predecessors, Alfred Thayer Mahan, talked about national power in complimentary terms. He said that ". . . the purpose of power is to permit moral ideas to take root."

We'll be discussing the naval power of the Soviet Union and how it stacks up with that of our Navy now and in the future. This subject is very difficult to sort out in the American press and in American discussions because in the last decade we seem to have burdened ourselves with a national self-consciousness that has become a self-inflicted wound of guilt, a national shame at being strong. Moreover, we have assigned ourselves this shame at the very time our relative advantage of power in the world has dropped out from under us. I'd like to suggest that nowadays a more accurate assessment of the balance of power between the United States and the Soviet Union can be obtained from foreign, third-power sources than from our countrymen. We might find not only a more accurate appraisal of the balance, but very likely a more important one because perceptions of power, rather than proven power itself, are what actually determine the occurrence of war or peace.

I had one good look at the foreign perception of the balance at a conference at Oxford University last fall. It was at the annual meeting of the International Institute of Strategic Studies. One hundred scholars and statesmen attended: a handful of Americans, the bulk West German, French and British. All were men of established reputations as experts in international affairs. The subject of the conference was the power and posture of the Soviet Union in the 1980s. Some of the American intellectuals present were shocked to observe that their European counterparts, many of a social-democratic political persuasion, uttered not one word advocating the appeasement or even accommodation of the Soviet Union during the week of discussions. They offered instead a litany of consternation and concern about the future implications of a U.S./USSR defense outlay imbalance by which for over a decade Russia has spent half again as much as the U.S. for finished ships and battlefield equipment, and twice as much for military research and development. In addition to the hardware picture, time and again these Europeans voiced anxiety over the emerging leadership of the Soviet Union in the decade ahead.

Dr. John Erickson of Edinburgh University was one of several who pointed out that high military rank in the Soviet Union even now depends upon a good World War II combat record. Moreover, most of those in positions of high political responsibility were early in their lives close enough to the old Bolsheviks to have adopted not only their skill and cunning, but some of their idealism as well. What those Europeans at Oxford feared most was the replacement of these old-timers with shallow, glib, frustrated technocrats who very likely will have neither the restraint that comes with prolonged experience in the management of power nor the idealism (perverted perhaps, but real) of their predecessors. This year's President of IISS, the old

French philosopher, historian and analyst of world affairs, Raymond Aron, has recently written that Russia is without doubt the number one military power in the world. He says that the spectre haunting Europe is no longer communism, but the Russian (not Soviet) military machine.

This carefully phrased distinction between a discredited communist power, borne on a wave of history, and a real nationalistic Russian power borne on a wave of rockets was a basic theme of another third party assessment recently received. This assessment came from a group located east of Europe and was printed in the March 31 edition of the liberal *New Republic* under the title "Spengler in Moscow (The Decline of the West)." An anonymous American author spoke for a new breed of Moscow intellectuals, those who are conscious of the cynicism of their government and yet not dissidents in the sense that they have any plan or potential to oppose it. These are the swingers of Moscow who stay abreast of the American disco scene and read the writings of the likes of historian Roy Medvedev, the Kremlin's loyal opposition who criticizes the scene from a Marxist viewpoint. The article is a story of lament, lament of the inevitable holocaust ahead. These Moscow intellectuals seem to have resigned themselves to a sort of Pascal's wager, a wager by which they would lose the least if their best guess were wrong, a wager on World War III. They profess to rather like Americans, and they laughed at Khrushchev's remark, "We will bury you." They regret that the remark could truthfully be made now for reasons of power in existence rather than power in a mystical theory of history. To them, it is only natural that a U.S.-China alliance be formed, because as they see it, it would be absurd for the United States to dare to oppose Russia alone.

The thing that has crystallized the alarm of these Marxist intellectuals, however, is not so much the real power balance per se as the worldwide perception of a weakness and lack of will on the part of the West. They cannot, really cannot, understand how America could become so sensitive to sideline heckling and so fickle and faint-hearted as to drop the ball game in Vietnam. Neither can they believe the success, the unopposed success, of their own government's recent thrusts into Asia and Africa. The *New Republic* article describes their depression at seeing international instability being triggered by what they perceive as America's naive notion that appeasement is the road to peace.

I've spent a good bit of my life being dragged out of bed and being battered around every morning by men who shook their fingers at me and said, "The blood is on *your* hands." It's almost amusing to read today how Marxist intellectuals are charging American public figures with causing a world destabilization, telling them that the holocaust to follow will be "blood on their hands."

TAKING STOCK _____

Naval War College Review, May–June 1979

A few months ago *The New York Times* carried an article entitled "The Leveling of America." It was written by William Manchester, a faculty member of Wesleyan University and author of the recent biography of Douglas MacArthur, *American Caesar*. In this article Manchester lamented America's preoccupation with idolizing equality and shunning any recognition of human excellence. He said we had all joined a gigantic cult of American egalitarianism, a cult that is a sort of secular religion, a religion worshiping human mediocrity, a religion that had become just as powerful and intolerant as 17th century New England Puritanism. Manchester refers not to that social equality of access recognized as an American's right, but rather to that equality that results when our humanness—our goals, achievements, personal standards, rewards—is reduced to the lowest common denominator. I share his view; the "Leveling of America" type of equality is evil and flies in the face of our national and even our Western heritage.

The American idolatry of self-deprecation, this reverence of a mediocre base has been with us for about two generations. (Manchester found its beginnings in the immediate post–World War II period.) In our lifetimes that trend grew into a national fetish that confused equality with blurred distinctions between generations, sexes, classes, and achievements. The term *elitism* became a commonplace epithet used to scorn or berate any program advocating competitive excellence or even providing recognition for those who exceeded the norms of the group. In our schools it led to the sanctification of "relevance" (to be defined by the consumer, of course), and that became a capitulation to the shallow, to a new sophism in which the traditional academic pursuit of human knowledge was all but lost; credits were given for casual studies that didn't qualify as disciplines; academic offerings resembled a smorgasbord instead of an ordered coherent pattern of learning; academic rigor was trampled by the haste and barbarism of specialization. Equality manifested itself in an "egalitarianism of ideas"; this led to an ideology of relativism that tolerated—even honored—a lack of discrimination in thought that opened the door to an undisciplined cant and to a political opportunism that horrified those of sober reflection as much as it would have horrified the classical Greeks.

In recent months, we have begun to see a turning away from all this, at least in the field of higher education. This is not to say that our society has not been blighted by the equality binge, but I rejoice in the fact that that blight is beginning to be stripped away by a regenerative, stronger force. As Hegel would say, we are at that point of synthesis in the dialectical process; we are at the point of a pivotal swing in the trends of education. Harvard introduces its "core curriculum" this fall, abandoning the broad, general introductory courses and substituting a list of highly specific subjects that set tougher standards for graduation. Moreover, recent articles from the west coast pacesetter, Stanford, have highlighted campus enthusiasm for a return to the classics and to a reconsideration of those timeless documents that really said it all—those guideposts that were sadly ignored by those seeking new solutions to new problems. In my view, new problems (if any problem really is new) should be candled against the light and wisdom of the classical thinkers who conceived the disciplines that mankind, over the centuries, has used profitably to solve them.

In good times we seem to be able to get by with liberal doses of mediocrity born of equality but in adversity we crave that excellence born of unfettered human freedom. Freedom is necessary for excellence, and discipline is necessary for freedom. Dedication to excellence through the entire range of behavior pays significant dividends in the good times and the bad, for the things we practice until they become habit form the foundations of character. Goethe once wrote that you limit a man's potential by appealing to what he is; you must appeal to what he might be. Mediocrity should describe the lower limit of our behavior, not the norm. There are too few people in uniform today who are willing to apply themselves to the demands that a commitment to excellence entails. Excellence is as necessary to the military man as armament, for without it you're losing the battle before you've engaged the enemy.

The leveling of America had no biological roots, rather it was a self-inflicted wound. Similarly the drive for excellence is born of the human will. Civilization is but a thin veneer on society, and we are but one generation removed from barbarism. In times ahead people will look to excellence, look to those who actively and faithfully preserve this precious thin veneer. They will hug to their breasts the kind of inspired excellence needed to hold order, coherence, and culture together. Many of those with that excellence will be in uniform. Complacency does not complement that uniform, nor does satisfaction with egalitarianism.

☆

While at the Naval War College I visited and spoke at all three Service Academies. For this group of writings, I have chosen one I gave at West Point. Their incoming freshman class hears three major talks during their indoctrination summer. One is on "Duty," one on "Honor," and one on "Country." In the summer of 1979, I gave the first.

DUTY

Address to the Class of 1983, United States Military Academy, West Point, July 13, 1979

The subject tonight is *duty* and I'm going to begin with a Naval reference. Don't be alarmed at the navy film, and now a naval story. Duty for us all is the same; moreover, half the philosophy students you saw in my class at the War College are Army officers. I was in prison with Marine, Air Force and Army officers and I am not parochial.

So I would like to begin this discussion of duty with a well-known British admiral's flag hoist signal to his fleet as they closed on the enemy to commence the Royal Navy's most famous battle. It was, of course, Lord Horatio Nelson's signal before the Battle of Trafalgar, a signal that history has shown to be the beginning of the end of Napoleon's hope to dominate Europe by force. The ultimately victorious Admiral Nelson had ordered the hoisting of flags which said simply this:

> England expects that every man will do his duty.
> England expects that every man will do his duty.

That signal is a short but complete lesson in the fundamental and necessary concept of *duty*, a lesson I hope you cadets will long remember. One important thing to remember is that it was given by a man in uniform.

Take note of the important word "expects" in Nelson's signal. The idea of expectation is very much a part of the concept of duty.

The old Greeks understood this notion of expectation. They had a word for what we call virtue or moral excellence: *arete*. To the Greeks a good man was a man who did what was *expected* of him depending upon his particular station in the world.

A good cobbler was one who was expected to produce well-made shoes. And this was reiterated by Plato and Aristotle.

One should expect a good navigator, then and now, to guide his ship safely over the sea and into harbor.

A good soldier, as Aristotle in particular emphasized, was one who could be expected to display certain characteristics on the battlefield: courage, obedience, loyalty, steadfastness, resourcefulness. Courage (or the Greek word *andreia*, a synonym for manliness) was the first virtue of a man as well as of a soldier. Plato defines courage as endurance of the soul. The Greeks stressed endurance; they admired a man who could give the quick thrust, the audacious dash, but they reserved their highest praise for the man who "hung in there" battling against the terrible odds, the nearly certain defeat. A more modern military leader, Frederick the Great, took as his personal watchword the command "Stand fast!"

Finally, a good man to the old Greeks was a man who could be expected to display those virtues of character proper to a human as a human, not just his occupational standards as a cobbler, or as a navigator, or as a soldier.

The stoic philosophers, most of whom lived right after the heyday of the Greeks, illustrated this idea of expectation in the moral life by the metaphor of the actor, of the stage, of the drama. Men and women are called on in life to play a part. The part may be a big one or a small one, but once the part is given to us on life's stage, it is expected of us to play it well. In Hanoi's prisons at times when I was so depressed that military virtue seemed almost at the point of irrelevance, I was comforted and strengthened by remembering Epictetus' admonition (and I *did* remember it—as I've written, Epictetus' *Enchiridion* was one of my prize memories) "Remember that you are an actor in a drama of such sort as the Author chooses—if short, then in a short one; if long, then in a long one. If it be his pleasure that you should enact a poor man, or a cripple, or a ruler, or a private citizen, see that you act it well. For this is your business—to act well the given part, but to choose it belongs to another." You young men and women of this West Point Class of 1983 have been given a part and your part is that of a military officer. Your duty is doing what is expected of you. You are *expected* to play your part well.

So was it for Lord Nelson, and he played his part well. Courage? He lost an eye in one action and his right arm in another and still fought his greatest battles in the seven years that followed. Nelson's first thought was for his men. Wounded in action as a young officer, he refused to let the surgeons tend to him first. He was famous for saying that he would take his turn with, as he said, "his brave fellows."

Robert Southey published his *Life of Nelson* just eight years after Nelson had been mortally wounded and died in his flagship HMS *Victory* as he turned the tide at that Battle of Trafalgar, the same day he hoisted that signal about expecting Englishmen to do their duty. Southey tells us,

> Never was any commander more beloved. He governed his men by their reason and their affections; they knew that he was incapable of caprice or tyranny; and they obeyed him with alacrity and joy, because he possessed their confidence as well as their love. "Our Nel" they used to say, "is as brave as a lion, and as gentle as a lamb." Severe discipline he detested, although he had been bred in a severe school (he went to sea when he was 12); he never inflicted corporal punishment if it were possible to avoid it. And when compelled to enforce it, he, who was familiar with wounds and death, suffered like a woman. In his whole life, Nelson was never known to act unkindly towards an officer. In Nelson there was more than easiness and humanity of a happy nature: he did not merely abstain from injury; his was an active and watchful benevolence, ever desirous not only to render justice, but to do good.

Such was the character of the officer who expected every man under his command to do his duty, as he himself surely always did.

The concept of duty is not popular today in some circles. We live in a world of social turmoil and shifting values, a world where people insist on their rights but often ignore their duties. So great is the concern for rights today that people will invoke the total machinery and full power of the law to secure those rights. As a result, our nation in my view is choked with legalism, a situation that even a distinguished persecuted foreigner thought dangerous enough to bring to our attention. Of course I'm talking about Solzhenitsyn in his Harvard commencement address a year ago, when he warned that our nation had shifted the focus from the substance of the good to the rule book of rights. In this he saw the beginning of the decline of our nation's strength and national will. And I agree with him. Unless we are willing to balance each of the rights we claim with a correlative duty, we'll be as a nation like the man who wants a dollar's pay but is not willing to do a dollar's worth of work to get it. Rights incur obligations.

You of the military profession, although just initiated, will soon feel the weight of this responsibility and must lead the way in awareness of the crucial importance of duty. You must be not only leaders to your men but examples to the nation of the truth that for any position of responsibility in society, whether it be in the family, government, business, or military, there is a corresponding obligation to carry out the assigned task.

Where did this idea of duty come from? What are its historical roots? In his book *Essay on Human Understanding*, the 17th-century philosopher

John Locke discussed the simple question, "Why a man must keep his word." He found three different answers to this question; answers that I believe are as applicable today as they were then.

First, said Locke, a Christian man will say, "Because God who has the power of eternal life and death requires it of me that I keep my word."

Secondly, said Locke, if one takes the Hobbesian view of life, he will say, "Because society requires it and the state will punish you if you don't." (Hobbes was a very practical kind of hardnosed guy.)

And thirdly, John Locke observed that had one of the old Greek philosophers been asked why a man should keep his word, the latter would say, "Because not to keep your word is dishonest, below the dignity of man, the opposite to virtue (arete)."

Two of the answers Locke cites, the Christian and the Hobbesist, seem to derive duty from the command of law, external law, the law of God in one case, the law of the state in the other. But the third answer, the Greek answer, shows that duty can be understood without reference to external law or to compulsion, divine or human. We share this understanding whenever, having made a promise, taken an oath, contracted a debt of duty—as you cadets have recently done—we feel an obligation to discharge it, even if no superior commands the act. Duty in this perspective has an absolute character. Duty is its own justification. It does not have to be propped up by anything outside itself, particularly in the line of reward or punishment. This was the teaching of Socrates who urged that men should obey the law, pay their debts, discharge their obligations, not to avoid the pain of censure or punishment, but simply because they ought to.

Closer to our own time, the great German philosopher Immanuel Kant said much the same thing. Kant was a very bright man. Known generally as a moral philosopher, he gave us much more. He really explained the function of the human mind. Moral obligation in his view rests on an internal conviction of duty, the law we give to ourselves from ourselves, conscience if you like, and not the law that pressures us from the outside government. To Kant carrying out our moral obligation is obeying the law we set each for ourselves. He happened to be a religious man but he was very careful in his instruction never to rely on religion as a justification for any of his ideas; he relied only on what he called pure reason. The law we set for ourselves is *free* in contrast with the external law which is *compelling*, said Kant. The argument echoes the age-old irony of the necessity of discipline for freedom. That internal law we may call the voice of conscience. It is the inner awareness of what our duty is, and it rests on no foundation but itself. The obligation to do our duty is *unconditional*. That is, we must do it for the sake of duty, because it is the right thing to do, not because it will profit us psychologically or socially or economically, not because if we don't do it and get caught we'll be punished. The categorical imperative was Kant's name for this inbred, self-imposed restraint, for the command of conscience within that tells us that the only true moral act is done from a pure sense of duty. So you can't ask what benefits will accrue from performing your duty. You must do your duty because it *is* your duty. Period. Simply put, that is the concept I want to leave with you and there's plenty of intellectual background to support it.

I hope this posits the concept of duty in historical perspective. But Locke and Kant may seem a long way from the officer (very likely many of you), soon perhaps to be standing in front of a platoon or leading a group of men in harm's way, into this very peculiar enterprise we call war. On the battlefield, you very well may find yourselves in new decision-making territory where all previous bets are off, where the rational, managerial approach of many of our fathers is no longer valid. I am describing that duty of arms that Clausewitz described as "a special profession . . . However general its relation may be and even if all the male population of a country capable of bearing arms were able to practice it, war would still continue to be different and separate from any other activity which occupies the life of man." Another old warrior, William Tecumseh Sherman (just 143 classes ahead of you plebes here tonight), said, "War is cruelty and you can't refine it."

The duty of uniformed men has a long, colorful, and frequently bloody history, and it will be no different in the future. Those who think that we've seen our last war are, in my opinion, dead wrong. I make a Pascal wager that a general war will blight this planet, probably before the end of the century. Pascal, of course, advised us all to wager on that outcome by which one would stand to lose the least in case we were wrong. The trends as I read them make war the safer wager.

A lot needs to be said about the kind of education most appropriate for the professional soldiers you have chosen to be in these times of impending peril. You must aspire to a strength, a compassion, and a conviction several octaves above that of the man on the street. You can never settle for the lifestyle that Joseph Conrad characterized as ". . . skimming over the years of existence to sink gently into a placid grave, ignorant of life to the last, without ever having been made to see all it may contain of perfidy, of violence, and of terror . . ."

How to avoid ignorance of perfidy, of violence, of terror? Your education must include those intense emotional experiences of the sort common here. You will leave this place with more than a diploma. You will likely leave it with a highly developed conscience. It's almost impossible to graduate from an institution like this without it. You will have undergone an irreversible process which will never again allow you the comfort of self-satisfaction while being glib or shallow. You will likely forever carry the burdens, and they are burdens, of loyalty, commitment, passion and idealism. You will have undergone an education of the sort people refer to when they say that education is what's left over after you've forgotten all the facts you learned. And that which is left over, that conscience, that sentiment, is indispensable to that capability for which the graduates of this institution are known. And that capability is leadership.

Here at West Point, you'll learn the range of responsibility that a commitment to duty demands. Some of the things a good leader with a strong sense of duty is expected to do may surprise you. I'd like to examine some of the seldom mentioned obligations of an officer.

I say it's your duty to be a moralist. I define the moralist not as one who sententiously exhorts men to be good, but one who elucidates what the good is. (Under the press of circumstance this is sometimes unclear—perhaps in a prison camp.) The disciplined life *here* will encourage you to be men and women of integrity committed to a code of conduct and from these good habits a strength of character and resolve will grow. This is the solid foundation from which you elucidate the good, by your example, your actions and your proud tradition. A moralist can make conscious what lies unconscious among his followers, lifting them out of their everyday selves, into their better selves. The German poet Goethe once said that you limit a man's potential by appealing to what he is; rather, you must appeal to what he might be.

Secondly, there are times when you'll have to act as a jurist, when the decisions you'll make will be based solely on your ideas of right and wrong, your knowledge of the people who will be affected, and your strength of conviction. There won't be a textbook or school solution to go by. I'm talking about hard decisions when you'll be the one with a problem that has seemingly endless complications—when you'll have to think it through on your own. As a jurist, you may be writing the law, or at least regulations, and that's a weighty responsibility. When you're in the hot seat, you'll need the courage to withstand the inclination to duck a problem or hand it off; you've got to take it head on.

One word of caution: Many of your laws will be unpopular. You'll have to learn to live with that. But your laws should never be unjust. Moreover, you must never cross that fatal line of writing a law that cannot be obeyed. You must be positive and clear and not lapse into a bureaucratic welter of relativism that will have others asking what you *really* mean or trying to respond in the most politically acceptable way.

And you'll find it's going to be your duty to be a teacher. Every great leader I've known has been a great teacher, able to give those around him a sense of perspective and to set the moral, social and particularly the motivational climate among them. You must have the sensitivity to perceive philosophic disarray in your charges and to put things in order. A good starting point is to put some time in on that old injunction, "Know thyself."

Here at West Point you will follow in the footsteps of greatness. During your years here, I challenge you to leave those same clear footprints for future generations to follow. In John Ruskin's words such a process is "painful, continual and difficult . . . to be done by kindness, by waiting, by warning, by precept, by praise, but above all by example." Teachership (in my view) is indispensable to leadership and an integral part of duty.

Fourth, you must be willing to be a steward. By that I mean you must tend the flock as well as crack the whip; you have to be compassionate and realize that all men are not products of the same mold. The old Civil War historian Douglas Southall Freeman described his formula for stewardship at my school, the Naval War College, thirty years ago last month. He said you have to know your stuff, to be a man, and to take care of your men. There are flocks outside these walls that will require your attention and test your stewardship. They're not all West Pointers out there.

The final duty is that you must be able to act as philosophers in your careers in order to explain and understand the lack of a moral economy in this universe. Many people have a great deal of difficulty with the fact that virtue is not always rewarded nor is evil always punished. To handle tragedy may indeed be the mark of an educated man, for one of the principal goals of education is to prepare us for failure. When it happens, you have to stand up and cope with it, not lash out at scapegoats or go into your shell. The test of character is not "hanging in there" when you expect a light at the end of the tunnel, but performance of duty and persistence of example when you know that no light is coming. Believe me, I've been there.

☆   ☆   ☆   ☆   ☆

And now I'll take some questions.

Q: Sir, New Cadet Downing, 8th Cadet Basic Training Company. Sir, could you give us, the Class of 1983, some helpful advice on how we might get through the next four weeks of cadet basic training?

A: I'll tell you, by the time Christmas leave rolls around, you'll remember this summer with fondness. I am confident that you are all up to it or you wouldn't have been admitted to this fine company of men and women. I can remember many of my midshipman days, under the same type of pressure you're getting, with great fondness. Some of the tests, some of the little and not so little challenges that you face of a physical nature—swimming the extra length or going the extra round of boxing, are comforting later. It gives one confidence to have mastered physical challenges. That knowledge will give you strength in future tests. You are manufacturing here, in these years at West Point, dreams that you are going to carry into your old age. Nothing was more obvious to me in prison than that one of our primary tasks in life is to collect worthwhile memories, fuel for good dreams. Memories of good friends of whom you are proud are precious in solitude. I was alone for four and a half years and I didn't have anything to go on but my memories and I really sorted out the good and the bad. I fancied myself as having a practice run at growing old. If you do anything of which you are ashamed, it becomes a cancerous sore that you have to somehow accommodate in your loneliness (or in old age). But the good stuff, running the race well, will sustain you.

Q: Sir, Cadet Smith, 4th Cadet Basic Training Company. Sir, with your record in Vietnam as a prisoner of war, to what do you attribute your ability to escape death at the hands of the North Vietnamese with your activities that helped inspire all Americans over there to resist them?

A: I was just lucky enough to be a senior man in the company of some great Americans, off-the-shelf Americans. The decision of who got in there was made by random selection. I'm not giving you just my viewpoint, I'm giving you the distillation of the viewpoints of most of my close and senior friends: You don't work against a threshold of pain problem so much as you work against a courage problem. Success came to be measured not by the pain you could absorb in a given instance, but by your repeated courage to make them hurt you each time before you gave them anything. That did a lot of good. It gave them never ending trouble.

We saw the value of the thing I was talking about, the Greek ideas of endurance. I've seen that proven to be the real measure of the man and the real key to moral victory because this deteriorated the Vietnamese confidence and it improved our self-respect. It eliminated, for us, any problem of guilt because we had done the best we could. This very important idea was never formally codified, but it became custom. Another thing that grew by custom and was very important was to level with your fellow Americans under all circumstances. Everybody was always terribly depressed the first time he was forced to degrade himself. He had in his mind that he had failed. He had succumbed to pain and he had said that he bombed churches, schools, and pagodas or whatever the current phrase was. It was really damaging to a man, particularly if he couldn't fight back. What was really damaging was withholding this information, not letting fellow Americans know it. We made a practice anytime we came back from an interrogation by the enemy, to level with our people, to tell them what information we had given up. (It might be where the notes were dropped, it might be a code, it might be this or that.) It got rid of that guilt. That's what really tears you apart, there's where the real problem occurs, when you allow yourself to be scared or guilt-ridden. If you realize fear and guilt are your enemies, and not pain, then you've got a ticket to self-respect and certainly to friendship and support of your fellows. I'm not just telling you how to behave in prison, I'm telling you how to stay out of the grips of bureaucratic or any kind of extortion, how to avoid being used, how to rely on your conscience, how to keep your self-respect. You've got to start right off by unloading to and confiding in and trusting your fellow officers and your men.

Q: Sir, New Cadet Resparsky, 7th Cadet Basic Training Company. Sir, did you ever find it necessary to think of when the end would come to your prison sentence or did you live on a day to day basis?

A: Well, I lived on a day to day basis. I was a pessimist. Of course we had to communicate by tapping on walls, and there was a lot of communication going on in our supposedly silent world. When I say communication, I mean conversation, not just signals and grunts. We pretty well knew each other's outlook and most guys thought it was really better for everybody to be an optimist. I wasn't naturally that way; I knew too much about the politics of Asia when I got shot down. I think there was a lot of damage done by optimists; other writers from other wars share that opinion. The problem is, some people believe what professional optimists are passing out and come unglued when their predictions don't work out. Over time, we started getting a boost out of our bad luck. I can remember Howie Rutledge saying, "Talk about World War II, I've been in solitary confinement longer than World War II lasted." So we made destitution a prestige item. Most Americans, once they had invested so much time in there, didn't want to come home under any conditions short of total honor and victory. When George McGovern said he would go to Hanoi on his knees, we prisoners in Hanoi were humiliated. We did not go anywhere on our knees, least of all home. We were going to walk out of there like soldiers. This wasn't a big thing with us the first two or three years, but after eight years in that place we had the biggest bunch of hawks in the world. Most of us would be there now rather than knuckle under.

Q: Sir, New Cadet Griffith, 1st Basic Training Company. Sir, as a leader, which duty do you feel has first priority? Duty to yourself or duty to your men?

A: Duty to your men. I've got good examples of that. That was a choice, in Hanoi; that was a very big choice. One can rationalize it either way. A guy could say, "I'm a Colonel and I owe it to my government not to give up these secrets and not to make a political spectacle of myself so I'm just going to sit in here and take care of myself." A few thought that for a while. That's the wrong decision, almost all agreed before it was over. You've got to take your short-run losses and lead. Your main job as a line officer is leadership and you've got to be up front. You've got to get those men together and you've got to take lumps for them—anything else really tears you apart, because if you rot in solitude officers junior to you will be leading and being beaten up; they're trying to do right and they can't get ahold of the boss and pretty soon your reputation is shot, and nobody will respect you when you do speak up. I'm here to tell you that when you've got a choice between acting as a leader in accordance with your position in seniority and that means if you're the senior man you've got to be responsible for everything, or going it alone, staking out the optimum position for yourself, you're going to regret it. In prison I put out slogans, a lot of them, but one of them, the first one, was "BACKUS." Each letter had a special meaning but the "US" meant "Unity Over Self." The new guy coming in had to realize that if he was going to perform his duty to himself as the first priority, he was going to make out better, he was going to get hurt less, he was going to give up less. But that was not the way to go because *unity* was the thing; we had to all go together. They could not fight us together. But if guys were alone they could tear you all apart; they can pit one against another.

Nothing superseded their interest in destroying prisoner organizations. All that whole country's leadership had been in prison, the same cells we were in. When the French held the country, the communists were the underground guys and they were all in those cells. I have read propaganda leaflets about how the old communist prisoners defeated the French with unity. So they knew the secret to prisoner success. Once they knew that that camp was under control and that everybody was giving them the same answer and that some senior American was running the place, they dropped everything. Every show was off. They had a purge, they called everybody in, they beat them up until they found who the leader was.

And that was the name of the game. You had to build a society to have it torn down, and then rebuild, year in and year out. To stop was to reveal a fatal character flaw. They really knew all about that. It's the kind of common sense, street-fighting sense, that we've all got to understand. They would not accept us as military officers. So, you get the idea from that, that what really kills them, is the leadership. When the senior officer leads, they get set back, and they don't like it. I can remember one time being told by an officer on the Central Committee, if you will believe it, "You have set us back two years with your organization." I was more proud of that remark than anything I had ever heard because I had 300 guys that were ready to go the route together. That's what I was getting paid for, that's what you're getting paid for.

Q: Sir, New Cadet Stout, Cadet Basic Training Company Number 6.

Sir, do you feel your moral character and fortitude was developed thoroughly enough through your peacetime training to handle the pressures of war or was the training merely a base of operations from which to develop yourself as situations arose?

A: I think the core question there seemed to be, can virtue be taught? That question has plagued mankind for years. Plato was skeptical about it, Aristotle thought that it could be taught. I think it can be taught. And I think my Academy background was a very big plus. I think body contact sports helped me. I think that plebe year helped me. Then there is another aspect to Academy life, and that's pride. You've got to take a certain responsibility. You must not sell yourself short. You can take your course catalog and you can take your physical training program, and they're great, but if you try to totally justify a place like this from there, you sell it short because there's still another dimension and that dimension is the tradition. It's more than a tradition, it's an élan. Some critical day that will grab you and keep you from selling yourself short.

This was one of several talks I was invited to give to computer-communications engineers on the subject of the prison-proven intuitive ability of the human mind. The message to them was that they were overbuilding their very expensive Pentagon-to-foxhole two-way links. The writeup that follows won their professional association's prize for the best essay of the year.

COMMUNICATING
WITHOUT TECHNOLOGY _____

IEEE Aerospace and Electronic Systems Society Newsletter,
March 1980

Being President of the Naval War College is an exciting job. Throughout the academic year, I work with and teach some of the finest middle-grade officers of all the Defense Department services and selected civilian agencies. My summers are equally interesting. Last summer, we hosted the Defense

Reprinted from IEEE AEROSPACE AND ELECTRONIC SYSTEMS SOCIETY NEWSLETTER, Vol. 15, No. 3, March 1980. This article originally appeared in

Science Board and will do so again this year. This group of bright and exciting people can really raise some unexpected questions.

A year ago, I met with a mathematics professor from Massachusetts Institute of Technology who wanted to know if I had any evidence to support the idea that at the Battle of Trafalgar, Lord Nelson had used a tactical plan that anticipated a relationship between firepower and maneuver that was later formalized mathematically as Lanchester's Law. This information dumbfounded me. In the two-hour discussion that followed, I became acquainted with Lanchester (a mathematics professor, turned overaged infantry officer in World War I), and his Law. Sure enough, Lord Nelson's battle plan at Trafalgar seemed to match Lanchester's theory.

Other questions that have come up at such meetings have involved artificial intelligence. I have learned that theory holds that with artificial intelligence devices a man can interact with a data bank in natural language. This, of course, brings to my mind the likenesses and differences of computers and brains.

Since I teach a philosophy course at the War College, I tend to stress the differences between computers and brains. Communicators, electronics engineers and computer experts in this audience may be interested to know that I teach the principle that although a computer might be deemed a sort of mechanical or electronic mind, one should never conclude that the mind is merely a sophisticated computer. The difference is critical.

I think you can tell already that I am launching myself on a tack (a good-natured one I hope) which is calculated to challenge some of the ideas of the communications and computer professions as I understand them.

I think it was Immanuel Kant, who lived in the same era as George Washington, who best sorted out the computer and brain issue. He was an arbitrator who best handled or resolved the conflict between the rationalists (Rene Descartes was the archetype) and the empiricists (particularly David Hume). Hume thought that the mind worked on bits like a computer and the output of the mind was actually just rearranged inputs or rearranged bits.

Immanuel Kant said that the mind is more than a bit processor—it supplies creative ideas and interpretations. Kant's ideas on this came to be appreciated much later by the hard science communities of quantum mechanics and nuclear theory. As far as I know, his idea of how the mind worked has never been challenged by the scientific highbrows. Kant upgraded the human mind to a central position in the cosmos, by saying, "if you are look-

SIGNAL, the official journal of the Armed Forces Communications and Electronics Association, October 1979. Copyright 1979.

ing for order in the universe, it is not 'out there,' it is 'in here'—in the human mind."

One of our Naval War College visitors most closely associated with your profession is Bert Fowler of the MITRE Corporation. We have had some good long discussions about communications theory, or, as I understand it, "the ascription of meaning to sensory data."

That is what I want to talk about today.

My view of communications theory is critical of your profession not giving the human mind enough credit. The result is overbuilt, overpriced systems that disgorge bales of unnecessary data which have the ill effects of not only inefficiency, but also the encouragement of bad command habits among our officers in the field.

I am going to talk about communications theory in the context of a prison camp during the Vietnam War in which everybody lived in solitary confinement—a solitary confinement in silence in which the use of torture was a punishment for those who broke that silence to communicate with their fellows.

Our Vietnam enemies gave us two options to choose from—we could lie low and not communicate and go to seed over the years of silence and solitude or we could communicate as a matter of military duty and take our lumps. Myself and all those near me were clearly in the second camp. So the problem became how to communicate stealthily.

As a starter, of course, you secretly tap on walls. The Morse Code is no good—it soon becomes obvious that you cannot cope with the limitations of a bitonal system. It is just not practical because you have got to have a reliable, repetitive beat.

But how do you build a monotonal system? There are many ways you could apply monotonal systems to the descriptions of letters. I believe the most efficient is a method devised back in the days of the American Civil War. The system drops the letter "K" out of the alphabet (a "C" can always be used where you would use a "K" and the meaning is preserved), and with the resultant 25 letter alphabet, sets up a 5 × 5 matrix. The system is comprised of a line across the top where the letters "A," "B," "C," "D," and "E" are assigned beats (such as 1–1 for an "A"; 1–2 for a "B"; 1–3 for a "C"; 1–4 for a "D"; and 1–5 for an "E"). Using the same convention, on the second line five more letters are added: 2–1 for "F," 2–2 for "G" and so forth. It follows that the most inefficient letter to transmit is "Z," with a 5–5 beat. But this is about as good as you are going to be able to do with efficiency with one tone and 25 letters.

What I have discussed so far and throughout this recounting is all common sense, all human mind. The same also holds true for operating signals—you do not need many. I am sure if I put any number of you in a cubicle and gave you a contract to devise a system of operating (OP) signals you would produce a complicated and cumbersome cross-indexed monstrosity.

In our situation, we devised operating signals under pressure and under the threat of pain, with a real appreciation for safety and efficiency. We found that only four OP signals were needed. The first is one that says "no," "danger," "stop," or any connotation of the negative. For this you should use any "one" signal—a single thump, a single noise, a single flash, a single wave. The second necessary operational signal should say "yes," "go," "concur," "execute," "good." For this we used two of anything—the most efficient signal except for the single beat "no" signal. The third necessary signal is "repeat," which was three for us. And the fourth is "wait"—four beats or four what-have-you in our method.

In seven and a half years of communicating almost solely by some application of the 5×5 matrix, neither I nor any one of my 400 companions experienced a need for another operating signal. That fact alone could save millions of dollars today.

One quickly realizes that the need to protect the channel is paramount. If you have been in isolation for a period of months and maybe years (as I had been) and suddenly get back to the mainstream and want to establish contact, you learn to be cautious about rushing into conversation. You learn to slow down and, first, agree with your partner about danger signals; second, you must agree on a cover story if you are caught, and third, you need to decide on a backup communication system.

Taking the trouble in that first few minutes of contact to say what happens "when we lose this net" has saved me more than once. You might simply specify a bent wire that indicates a hiding place for a note or an alternate call-up procedure—simplicity will get you by, but to ignore the need to establish fallback procedures first can mean months of communications interruption.

You are probably wondering at this point, "How in the world do you learn this monotonal code with its matrix alphabet without prior knowledge?" That is a good question. It turns out to be more of a theoretical than a practical problem. Sometimes you can stick notes in bowls of rice scheduled to be served, sometimes you can whisper under doors. One of my friends knew the matrix format when he came into the cell block for the first time. He explained that he saw it while forced to lie on the floor in the torture room. The matrix was diagrammed on the bottom of a table with the admonition, "All prisoners learn this code."

In the more common case, the teacher had to wait until the new prisoner had overcome his initial fear of working the wall by brushing it or thumping it. (He would have been threatened with going through the torture cycle again if he broke silence.) The new prisoner had to decide to take a chance and hope that it was not a guard trying to trick him into violating the camp rules of absolute silence. For some to overcome such apprehension took months, for some days, and for a very few, hours.

Experienced men found that for the most sluggish student it was best to commence by tapping 26 times on the wall. In a matter of minutes, hours, days, or maybe longer (depending upon who the student was), the person on the other side realized that you were talking about an alphabet. He eventually made some kind of recognition signal of his own design and let you know he understood that another human was using an alphabet.

That is the start. Communication is fundamentally the connection of one brain to another and they are sensitive instruments. I stress this point throughout—do not sell your brain short, because it can do better than David Hume says and perform better than the artificial intelligence designers think it can.

Once the novice knows that you are talking about an alphabet, it is a good assumption that "A" is probably one beat and 26 is probably "Z." If this understanding was slow to develop, one way that was used was to send your partner an "8" and then a pause and then a "9." Eventually his mind lights up—"8," "9"; "H," "I"—"Hi!" Then you are in business—an inefficient business, but a corner has been turned in this brain-to-brain relationship. Now you can start the laborious hours and days of trying to describe the regular communications system by this very primitive code.

But how did we call them up? How did we "roger"? What was the procedure? The answer was that we borrowed from a very American rhythm pattern for a call-up signal: The "shave and a haircut." When an American hears "shave and a haircut," even if he has never thought of a code, he almost automatically lunges to the wall and supplies his "two bits." We rogered with a "2," a "yes" as an affirmative signal after each *word* was copied or understood (of course, with some of the words that were long, you could tap them off early once you were ready to "buy" on the basis of what you had heard).

A very primitive form of encryption thus developed from the early tapoff. The interloper who does not know your language and does not know what has transpired between your two minds and how well you understand one another cannot intercept. Abbreviations confuse him even more, and abbreviation patterns can change over time with any two partners.

A man who is granted a contract to come up with an abbreviation table would probably give you something that would have to be changed almost entirely after the first month of use. But abbreviations hammered out in the field are solid.

For example, frequently you had to use the word "think," which was shortened to "TK"—I could go on and give you hundreds more examples.

They grew up in different camps with substantial variations. As people were mixed and new tappers came on the other wall, it amounted to a system of dialects. Yet we became accustomed to one another's dialects easily. If we did not understand their abbreviation, we would not give them the "2" signal until they had spelled out the entire word.

What I have described thus far is a jam-free system that cannot be countered. First of all, you had the discrete signature of your partner—his individual style. For instance, no two people gave the old Steve Canyon flamboyant "Roger, Roger" exactly the same way because the tapper's personality came out. You could recognize your friend by the way he expressed the "Roger, Roger"—by the speed, the touch, and whether he meant "yes," "OK," "concur," or "good," "WILCO," "oh yeah?" or "yes sir" or whatever. I understand that the Soviets back up all of their telemetry nets with a key. I certainly understand why.

This matrix system lent itself to other applications such as a visual flash system. Also, every time a detailed man would sweep the courtyard, he would be sending out a regular newspaper. Snickers would be heard in the cell block and the guard would become rattled. Every time we swept our toilet buckets out we were acting as town criers. We even developed a vocal tap code—I gave credit to my classmate Jerry Denton for that. Ones or twos were made with coughs or sniffs. The number three was a throat clear; the number four was a hack, and number five was either an exaggerated sneeze or a spit, depending on the conditions.

For official traffic, the senior ranking officer insisted that all members memorize the message. That was our law, as nothing was written down, of course. We thus became acquainted with the storage capacity of our minds and how many words we could memorize. Of course, it placed a large weight on the message composer because he had to put things out in a logical pattern so that a reasonable man could memorize them handily.

I can remember one afternoon in the little prison nicknamed Alcatraz, where several of us spent a couple of years, and where I, as the senior officer, had been sending out a long series of messages concerning how we were going to combat what we called the Fink Release Program (this program was one people at home were supposed to think was a benevolent early release program, but it actually amounted to buying your way out by becoming a propaganda tool).

It was a complicated subject. I sent out six 50-word groups, flashing them on call across to Nels Tanner (I had to flash them because my cell was across the courtyard). After receiving each group, Nels would have to leave his place under the door where he had seen my finger, go to the wall and tap it out in both directions and come back under the door. It would take a couple of hours or more to get a 300-word message out to everyone composed well enough that they could all memorize it. I remember just before being put in irons for the night (as we were every afternoon at 4 P.M.), Nels was saying goodnight (GN), under the door as he always said to me. He added that he had handled about 5,000 words that day—that is a lot of traffic.

All of this was happening in a place like "Alcatraz" where eleven of us, each in a tiny cell, were supposedly being thwarted in our communication attempts by two armed guards, each constantly patrolling, listening, and trying to find if there were any unauthorized sounds about. This activity went on for years.

Cryptography got more sophisticated as we handled classified information. We had date-time groups and we would "slide" the alphabet; additionally, we used a matrix to develop a script that really looked like chicken tracks, rotating the axes depending on the day and the date. What I am saying is that if you take about five good commonsensical manipulations with some versatility (such as a rotating axis, a slide, and a convention for each day), and put them in series, you can come up with a code that cannot be broken. When I got home, I challenged the Defense Intelligence Agency to break a sample that was written out to demonstrate to them the strength of our system and they could not do it because there were just too many variables. This illustrates the point that the human mind can come up with combinations in 30 minutes that computers can never break.

Why did I say earlier that we as communicators, when immersed in the technical world, do not give enough credit to the human mind? First of all, we complicate matters by always looking for a perfect system. A perfect system serves an idiot—it is bound to be too complex. I think there is a lot of wisdom in old Admiral Gorshkov's maxim that "the best is the enemy of the good enough."

Secondly, I believe that an overblown communication capacity gives our military commanders bad habits. I recently told the Midshipmen at the Naval Academy in a speech that I think there is a greater possibility of their having to depend on their own initiative in an out-of-communications situation than was necessary for my generation, especially because of the probable difficulties of radio wave transmissions in nuclear clouds.

You have got to think through the possibility of a communications blackout, and this is difficult when our officers are brought up in an environment of total communications. I had more trouble in Hanoi (even with senior officers) wasting too much time trying to speculate about what they thought Washington would think of our policies because they had been conditioned by good communications for years to be ill at ease when they were not able to touch base with headquarters. Imagine it—we were in a position where we knew more about how to run a prison organization than anybody else in the world at that time and our conditioned officers were uncomfortable relying on their own spontaneity and intuition!

Thirdly, I badmouth your profession because it seems to ignore Shelling's and other strategists' admonitions to not forget the tactical advantages of being out of communication. Think about it. If it is patently clear to your adversary that you cannot receive a message, there is no way he can send you an ultimatum. There are advantages to a commander when his troops know he cannot be contacted. They cannot ask for relief.

The bottom line is that there is no question of the importance of the linking of human minds in the face of an adversary. Communication cannot be stopped as long as the will to communicate exists. It has been my observation that in this computer age of specialized technology, there is still no substitute for the power of the human brain in meeting a seemingly insurmountable challenge.

☆   ☆   ☆   ☆   ☆

Extracted from *Signal* with permission of The Armed Forces Communications and Electronics Association. Much of this material is also contained in "The Tap Code," in *Military Collector & Historian, Journal of The Company of Military Historians*, Winter 1979.

TAKING STOCK

Naval War College Review, July–August 1979

I don't believe anyone could read any of my articles of the past two years and reach the conclusion that systems analysts are my kind of guys. It may thus strike some readers as odd that I begin this final Taking Stock by advocating the application of the logic of the world's first systems analyst—the 17th century mathematician and founder of modern probability theory, Blaise Pascal. His logic, in the matter of how to resolve issues of vast import, was not to apply the conventional wisdom of suspending judgment until all the facts are in, but to choose (*wager* was the word he used) that outcome by which one stands to lose the least in case he's wrong. I don't think it's too whimsical or too insensitive to apply Pascal's wager to the number one dilemma of our age—the occurrence or nonoccurrence of global war in the decade or two ahead. I think Pascal would agree that the smart wager is that global war will occur.

To me this wager is more than a fail-safe precaution; all the trends are tracking steadily in the direction of that outcome. Destabilization is in the wind and it seems an inevitable fallout of every political viewpoint. The liberal press feeds us a daily fare of what they perceive as the destabilizing influence of hawkish policies. What about dovish policies? Even the liberal *New Republic* is publishing articles that make a case for the destabilizing effects of them. A recent issue featured an article describing the deep lament of Moscow intellectuals who fear that the Kremlin's perception of American indecision and weakness will result in Soviet provocation, in the reckless pressing of their advantage. These intellectuals were described not as dissidents, but as scholars and coffeehouse skeptics who are conscious of their government's cynicism, and incredulous of an America on which they depended to keep the power balance stabilized, an America too sensitive to sideline heckling and so fickle and fainthearted as to drop the ball game in Vietnam and elsewhere. They don't understand us and are dismayed at the probable destabilizing results of our growing reputation for caving in.

Given the political fact that wars and rumors of wars can be made to follow from the logical extension of either hard-line or soft-line policies (and the historic fact that war has blighted this planet in all but 268 of the past 4000 years), I think it was reasonable that while speaking recently in Annapolis I advised the midshipmen not to waste emotional energy on the twists and turns of every current event, "but to rest their nervous systems and gird their loins for World War III." Said another way, "put your money on the number dictated by Pascal's logic and concentrate on acquiring the traits you will need to meet the tests ahead."

A fallout of my philosophy course, "Foundations of Moral Obligation," has been the illumination of some seldom stressed aspects of leadership that may well be a part of those tests. I mean in particular those necessary in the new decision-making territory our middle and junior grade officers of today can expect to find themselves in before the turn of the century. The new territory might well be one of a nuclear war, one that lasts for months, one in which communication with deployed units may be intermittent or severed. There in the eye of the storm, leadership will entail many unique duties that will test and challenge. The ability of our leaders to function in such a do-it-yourself environment may influence the direction as well as the outcome of the battle, or perhaps the war.

☆   ☆   ☆   ☆   ☆

I think it is clear that in my view, education prepares men for leadership and survival. For the record, I am convinced that formal education is now more important than ever for those of us in uniform. Certainly we can all see clearly the side of Pascal's wager on which the Soviets come down. As revealed in a recent book, *The Armed Forces of the USSR* (written by an American military couple well acquainted in Moscow), Soviet officer education takes a top priority in professional development and the courses are continually being lengthened and made more rigorous. Today, a Soviet officer cannot be assigned command of an army brigade or higher, or command of a naval second rank ship or higher, unless he has had the rough equivalent of our Postgraduate School or War College. I say "rough equivalent" because their course lengths are longer. Their shortest war college (the General Staff Academy) is a two-year course; the shortest technical PG is three years, most are four and some are five. Moreover, entrance to these academies is gained only through competitive examination for which junior officers in their late twenties spend thousands of hours preparing.

The future will test this nation's leadership, its resourcefulness, its imagination, its dedication, its creativity and its will. To bring the point closer to home, it will probably give several of our mid-career officers of today one (and if they're lucky, two) chances for a moment of magnificence. May they all be preparing themselves for that moment. May they never sell themselves short.

BREAKING IN
AS A CIVILIAN
ACADEMIC

III. *By the time the previous article—my last column for the* NWC Review—*had gone to press in the summer of 1979, I had had my head turned by an offer to accept the presidency of a civilian college, The Citadel, in Charleston, South Carolina. I retired from the Navy and took over the college presidency at the end of the summer of 1979. By the time this article appeared a year later as the cover story of* Parade Magazine, *I realized I had made a mistake. I found the intellectual atmosphere wanting; the hazing of freshmen was out of bounds. I was not willing to invest years of administrative maneuvering to overcome the inertia of those who had allowed this deterioration to take place. Others might relish such a challenge, but I had had my share of that sort of thing and wanted to get on with something more stimulating.*

I wanted to spend my time writing and teaching. A fellowship residency at the Hoover Institution, perhaps within the next year or so, might provide the opportunity.

FREEDOM: OUR MOST PRECIOUS NATIONAL TREASURE

Parade Publications, Inc., June 29, 1980

Before the big iron gates slammed behind me as I entered the Hanoi prison, I found it hard to think of freedom as something other than an abstraction that's used in songs, Supreme Court debates and political speeches. In this respect I was like many Americans today who take freedom for granted. By the time I was released to come home nearly eight years later, freedom had long since ceased to be an abstraction to me.

To those of us who have served time in Communist jails, freedom has a delicious, tangible meaning. It has become something we can figuratively reach out and touch. Such feelings are likely understandable in men who have spent years shackled and manacled in isolation. But my love of freedom is not just a reaction to cruelty; my appreciation of its preciousness stems from a first-hand understanding of its rarity. The void of freedom in other parts of the world—and particularly the passivity with which this lack is accepted—is staggering to a man who is born and raised free. In my Hanoi cell, I found myself daily picking up shocking signals in that milieu of deadened sensitivites. Like these:

—The routine feedlot attitude of the simple peasant guards who delivered daily food rations down the line to cooped-up humans, fowl and livestock, with expressionless unconcern for the continual darkness, suffocating closeness, and isolation in which the chickens, pigs and men were confined.

—The continuous barking of loudspeakers on the street telling the people of Hanoi what to think.

—The pathetic ignorance behind the outburst of a prominent political cadre who shouted to me in a moment of exasperation: "We may not have freedom, but after 4000 years we have order, and we will settle for that."

These and countless other impressions drive home to me the fact that human freedom is not the way of the world. To be free to come and go, to choose your life's work, to go for the big bucks or selfless service, or to hit the road as a drifter—these are not open choices to most of the 4.5 billion souls on this planet. Human freedom as we Americans know it is available only to a steadily shrinking minority of people.

You don't know what freedom is until, for a starter, you live for several years in a box-cell 10 feet long and 4 feet wide. I was crouched in the corner of that cell when my guards caught me writing a note to one of my fellow

POWs. They were very mad about that note, so they took me from that box-cell to an even smaller, low-ceilinged outbuilding, a place we called Calcutta, and laid me on the floor in squeeze irons.

Fetters and jail take away your external freedom; you can't get up and go. But what about the freedom of your will and spirit? Our captors wanted to get at that more than anything. Not by brainwashing—I don't believe there is such a thing—it's a journalist's word. The real answer is simpler: it's pain. They tied your arms behind your back with ropes, shutting off circulation, and then violently and methodically tightened those ropes further, forcing your head down between your legs to produce claustrophobia. Death was not an option; there was only one way to stop it, and that was to say, "I submit."

In his *Nicomachean Ethics*, Aristotle points out the difference between acts done voluntarily and those under compulsion. But he adds that a measure of free choice may remain even in the severest extortion situations. We had many ways of clinging to that tiny residue of freedom in Hanoi. One way was the tap code. Although we were in solitary confinement we could surreptitiously communicate with one another, set up a chain of command, encourage the doubtful, console the depressed, comfort the hurt.

We figured out ways to prevent our captors from manipulating us into making photo and television propaganda for them. One way was to assume a character like an actor—a personality of unpredictability. Our captors did not hold with unpredictability. When they put an American pilot before the cameras, they wanted to be sure that his behavior was predictable. To sabotage that, when put under stress you could stage random scenes of emotional instability. You could throw chairs around and yell, "To hell with the torture." You had to be a good actor. If they thought you had not lost control of yourself but were putting them on, within minutes you could be back in the ropes sobbing like a baby. When you pulled off the act convincingly, they didn't like it. For then you were not useful as propaganda. They'd say, "This guy is not what we want to take downtown."

People have said to me, "I couldn't take a prison experience like you guys. You all must have had a tremendously high threshold of pain." But it was not a question of a high or low threshold of pain; it was a question of endurance. It didn't matter so much if you submitted under pain one day so long as you made them start all over again the next day. They didn't like to do that. So the thing was to cling to that tiny vestige of freedom it was in your power to hold.

That word freedom is crucial. Freedom does not exist because our Constitution says it should. Over the course of our country's history, people have constantly labored to keep freedom and have paid dearly for it.

Our Declaration of Independence of 204 years ago this week remains one of the most stirring documents in history, signaling a commitment to bear the responsibilities of protecting a way of life. After our bitter struggle for independence, brave and earnest men stepped forward to write our Constitution and formally frame the reasons for which we had fought that unpopular war against the British. No one had to remind our Founding Fathers of the cost. Fifty-six of them knowingly laid their lives, liberty and honor on the line when they signed that Declaration of Independence. And they paid their dues. In the ensuing war, nine were killed in action, five died as prisoners of war, twelve had their homes burned, several lost sons, one man's wife died in prison, and seventeen (including Thomas Jefferson) went broke. The legacy of these men was summed up very simply by Tom Paine: "Those who expect to reap the blessings of freedom must, like men, undergo the fatigue of supporting it."

This nation has come a long way since the drafting of the Constitution, and the milestones are littered with human sacrifice. We've fought wars around the globe in freedom's name and have paid a terrible price for our most fundamental national belief. Today, there are men and women who may lay down their lives for this country and the freedom for which it stands.

We all bear the painful costs of freedom. As we formally celebrate the commitment to break from England and to protect our natural rights, let's hug to our breasts our freedom—our most precious national treasure—knowing that it, like a child, is imperfect and demanding but undeniably good. Let's keep our centuries-old habit of protecting that child of America, that freedom. She's getting more rare and precious every day.

☆

I walked out the door of The Citadel with great relief, heading for a visiting professorship at Hampden Sydney College in Virginia, and then for the Stanford campus. Meg Greenfield of The Washington Post *asked me for an article about my abrupt resignation. Below is my reply, which she printed on her editorial page.*

WHAT IS WORTH
RESIGNING FOR? _____

The Washington Post, September 21, 1980

A few weeks ago I abruptly resigned from my post as a college president and walked off the campus feeling good about my decision. The sequence of events had been very straightforward. I had found conditions that I believed to be detrimental to students and unfair to faculty, conditions with which I did not wish to be identified. When it became clear to me that prompt reform was impossible, that my governing board's resistance to change would swallow me up and saddle me with a period of complicity, I checked out. End of problem.

The specifics are really not very interesting. They involve the control of hazing, the selection of students, the rigor of the curriculum, and such less important issues as organizational streamlining and so on. The interesting part has been the split in the reactions to my resignation among those generally on my side. The split cuts right down the age line. With a few notable exceptions, my elders say, "Regrettable. Too bad you couldn't work out a consensus, a compromise with your governing board." My younger adult friends sing a different tune: "Way to go!" "Stick it in their ear."

This is not the first time I've come across this new attitude, this new spirit in our educated men and women in their 20s and 30s. I don't write it off as a fallout of the 1960s, or as irresponsible exuberance of youth, or as a manifestation of inexperience. I think it is born of a new, responsible, awakening of moral sensitivity. I like it. My first brush with it came when I was president of the Naval War College. There I taught a course in moral philosophy and periodically required each of my students to submit a paper on the resolution of moral dilemmas he had experienced or observed or read about. The student picked the subject, but naturally in a course given in the 1970s to military officers and government civilians, educated men and women between 30 and 45, issues of the Vietnam War got a lot of play. The same difference of attitude between youth and age on how to deal with Catch-22 squeeze plays, how to deal with responsibility without authority, how to deal with being trapped in the rising waters of complicity without access to either faucet or drain plug, showed up in those papers.

An oft-chosen Vietnam dilemma along those lines was the problem of the on-scene military commander who was deluged by over-control and meddling from Washington. The older officer typically wrote: "Our commanders frequently could not do what they thought was right. They were forced to make continual compromises. Nevertheless, they had a lifetime of experience that their country needed and thus a moral obligation to hang in there and work it out. No purpose would have been served by their stepping down in protest." More than a few young bucks—Army, Navy, Air Force, Marines—had a different slant: "It was a bad show. No officer should let himself get trapped into compromising or waffling his principles. Any commander worth his salt so trapped should quit in protest."

Has my generation become hooked on collegial solutions, on keeping the lid on, on seeking a consensus, on making a deal to preserve unanimity? Corporate life, board life, hierarchical life breeds that slide to accommodation we are told is necessary to get something accomplished, and that invitation to moral weakness. If you don't think any weakness is incurred by having been conditioned to reasonable compromise, try living in a communist jail for a few years. There, all they want is for you to "be reasonable." The name of their game is extortion, and the source of their leverage lies in their imposition of feelings of fear and guilt. Step one is getting the American prisoner to make a deal, a reasonable deal; *any* deal will do for a start. From my own experience I can state that a Prisoner Interrogator's Handbook would list among suggested openers, "Let us reason together," "You Americans are a sensible, pragmatic people; meet us halfway."

I do not advocate a POW name, rank, and serial number stance at every board of directors meeting here at home. But neither do I advocate suppressing moral sensibility in the interest of cooperation—or tenure. Prof. Richard A. Gabriel of St. Anselm's College, a prolific writer on military ethics, points out in the May issue of *ARMY* magazine that over the last 20 years Canada has had 27 generals retire or resign in protest, while during the same period the U.S. Army has had one.

It's my guess that when today's American young people reach their peak, their statistics in this respect—in military, corporate, or academic life—will change. And that ain't all bad.

☆

An autumn 1980 trip to the Stanford Campus formalized my appointment at Hoover to take effect the following spring. On a soft October night at an Institution dinner party under the stars in their courtyard, I gave the following talk, which was reprinted later in National Review *magazine.*

TOWARD HONOR
OR EFFICIENCY

National Review, July 10, 1981

Twenty years ago last fall I was a U.S. Navy lieutenant commander, a fighter pilot just off carrier duty, when I started the most important years of study of my life here at Stanford and the Hoover Institution. In a rather loosely administered two-year postgraduate program I was simply given a blank check by the American Government, the only requirement being that I get a master's degree and take whatever courses I thought appropriate for a naval officer in the time remaining. For me, that came to about 125 quarter-hours, mostly in the humanities. Our government never spent any money more fortuitously, and fortunately. Within three years of leaving Stanford, I had been shot down over North Vietnam, imprisoned in an old French dungeon in Hanoi, and was becoming the head-of-government of a covertly organized colony of American prisoners of war—a colony destined to remain autonomous for nearly eight years.

Mark Van Doren of Columbia University used to tell his students that before proclaiming a man educated, one would ask this question about him: Could he re-found his civilization? The re-founding of a civilization became my lot, and this Naval Academy engineer thanked God for those 24 months of history, politics, and philosophy, at Stanford and Hoover, under the tutelage of teachers like Jack Bunzel, Peter Duignan, Steve Jurika, and Phil Rhinelander.

Perhaps I should explain how desperately we needed to re-found our own civilization in those prisons of North Vietnam. The Communist regime put each of us in solitary confinement in an attempt to sever our ties with one another and with our cultural heritage. This hits hard after a few months, particularly a few months of intermittent torture and extortion. In fits of depression a man starts seeing the bottom of the barrel and realizes that, unless he gets some structure, some ritual, some poetry into his life, he is going to become an animal. In these conditions clandestine encrypted tap-and-flash codes get improvised and start linking lives and dreams together. Then comes the need for common practice in united resistance, and, in due course, if things are working right, codified law commences to emanate from the senior prisoner's cell. The communication network strengthens the bonds of comradeship as over the months and years a body politic of common customs, common loyalties, common values takes shape.

Isolation seems to have some sort of a purifying effect on the soul: as time wears on, ever more high-minded discourse flows from hard-worked memories which dredge up recollections of the best from the educational backgrounds of their owners. Compassion fairly seeps through the walls as the familiar tapping style and mindset of the never-seen neighbor next door become a substitute for family. Morale is tied to the box-score of the continuous battle of wits and determination waged against the prison administration. The prisoner's underground, under the positive control of their senior, alternately plays for time, riots, and drives the interrogators up the wall.

Where else could a man better prepare himself for leadership in such a life than at the Hoover Institution? After lectures by Aleksandr Kerensky and courses with Bob North on comparative Marxist thought, I felt ten feet tall, even when forced to kneel before that irate political cadre. I could look him in the eye and quietly tell him: "Lenin didn't say that. You're a deviationist." (That was usually a quick and blessed ticket back to my cell.)

As I left Newport, Rhode Island, to come back here to talk to you about national defense, my War College friends advised me: "For God's sake, don't go out there and regurgitate a lot of data that every congressional staffer knows. Tell them what you really think victory or defeat, the success or failure of arms, ultimately depends on."

I believe all I read in the better journals: all our military material indicators are down. The United States is Number Two in the world in conventional forces for sure, and in nuclear forces very likely. The Department of Defense's so-called solutions to such inferiorities over the last few years have more often than not been buried both in high-risk technology and in the out-years of the budget. Neither high-risk nor out-years bode well for our national arsenal, and everybody knows it.

Dwindling forces and false official optimism bring up that most important aspect of our current dilemma: public confidence in our defense establishment is eroding. Opinion-makers have been concluding that military and civilian planners lack heart in what they're doing. They have been saying that every link in the defense chain—Congress, Pentagon, White House, civilian contractors—seems to be faking it. The fancy scenarios to which we are treated are seen all too frequently to wind up as just plain smoke.

I bring up the public perceptions of faking it, of smoke, of lack of heart precisely because forty years in uniform, and particularly that decade of war and life behind enemy lines, have taught me that more than any other factor, military success or failure depends on the moral sentiment, the ethos, the spirit of the man in the street.

That sounds preachy, doesn't it? Well, I'm in good company. Napoleon: "Sentiment rules the world, and he who fails to take that into account can never hope to lead." Pericles, honoring the military dead in his famous funeral oration: ". . . the important thing today is not to review the details of battles, but to discuss the *spirit* with which our country faces trials." In the last fifty years, have the American people ever yielded up the wherewithal for winning in the absence of a grassroots sense that their society and its institutions had a special value?

Let me tell you, in a Communist country at war, in a Communist city under siege, nothing takes precedence over public support of national policy. We know, of course, that it's a force-fed system; Lenin rigged it that way. The point was not only that the nightly sings, the bribe-proof guards, and their diligent work on their patriotic essays would seem to indicate close coordination between national sentiment and military policy; it was the Party's intimacy with and influence over the man in the street. You have to give the old Bolsheviks credit for designing the whole state system around a Party whose job it is to track and steer the confluence of public sentiment and policy.

Midge Decter in a recent article contrasts the effort Communist countries make to monitor deep-rooted public sentiment toward public policy and the way the United States has let the two get more and more out of phase over the past quarter-century. Perhaps this is partly because we have become hooked on opinion polls. Their coarse measurements are more or less adequate for data on people's preferences on particular issues. But, Miss Decter says, normal everyday opinion polls are not adequate for ferreting out deep moral sentiment, that ethos which is individually divulged only over time and usually in heart-to-heart associations. The sentiment that counts lies beneath opinions on issues; it is too fine-grained for polls or voting booths. But if it is ignored and kept isolated from the light of political attention, it ". . . will fester in the nether regions where ideas circulate and grow powerful and then become distorted and poisonous."

The classic modern example of this was the tone-deafness and myopia of Lyndon Johnson and his gang of systems analysts at the outset of public disenchantment with the Vietnam War. The Johnson Administration was at first insensitive to the discontent, and then inept at making an early explanation of what was going on. I was in combat and prison when that nether region vortex got going in America, but I had a front-row seat in North Vietnam when the Communist world started watching and enjoying our leaders' belated recognition of the problem and then their overreaction to it. If spontaneous poster-making at the private soldier level can be considered the ultimate indicator of national elation, then that winter morning in 1968 when prison guards were setting off firecrackers and displaying crude sketches of a teary-eyed McNamara leaving the Pentagon for the World Bank had to be their counterpart of VJ Day.

That was about the time when most of the Democratic hawks started becoming chickens. I was in leg-irons in cell 13, Alcatraz prison, when the pidgin-English voice on the prison squawk box announced the appointment to office of a certain Defense Department Under Secretary. Two years later, while I was still in cell 13, still in leg-irons, the same pidgin-English voice announced, on the same cell loudspeaker, that Under Secretary's indignant resignation—and then went on to read excerpts from a book of "confessions" he had already written and distributed, describing his disillusionment with the war.

Did we in prison read this public turmoil in the way I'm sure the Vietnamese thought we would read it—as evidence of an unjust war? Certainly not. We read it as five years of inept national leadership—as executive failure to ensure that the public and the policy were in tune. Sensitivity to that interconnection comes naturally to a combat leader, particularly to a prison leader who has to build and tend his own infrastructure of support. James MacGregor Burns calls the type of leadership that is always needed in these cases, indeed needed in any political leadership job in times of stress, *transforming* as opposed to *transactional* (bargaining-table) leadership. Good leaders are *transforming* leaders who make themselves continually conscious of what is going on in the minds of their followers. They are able to do this at a level of sensitivity and with a timeliness that permits them to make subtle adjustments to policy when required, and subtle adjustments to the understanding and even the mindset of the man in the street, to match. Great leaders can implant high-minded needs in the place of self-interested wants in the hearts of their people.

Okay, you say, public sentiment is an important part of the national power equation. So, Mr. Self-Appointed Expert, how do you read that deep-seated American sentiment now? My answer is that, from talks on a hundred college campuses and meetings in a hundred community halls, I think that in America today the man in the street is frustrated by: (1) the belief that America is weakened to a point there she is no longer in control of her destiny, (2) the fact that he doesn't like this situation, and (3) the problem of his getting no satisfaction from abstract debates between high-level politicos, or from the indecipherable jargon of the Pentagon. Moreover, he is tired of wearing a hair shirt—tired of apologizing for America. He is willing to make more patriotic commitments than his political leaders over the last few years have felt they dared ask. What I see in him is not jingoism; it is neither exaggerated love of country nor doctrinaire hatred of the Russians. It is honest pride in a good and decent society.

Will Mr. Reagan be able to accommodate this sentiment as he sets our national course? You and I know that a change of thrust toward an American resurgence in the name of freedom would require at the very least a loud and clear public demand, no matter who is President. How could such a demand be generated?

With that rhetorical question, I could stop right now and let the whole thing stand as a sort of sketchily supported pep talk. I'm not going to do that. I'm going to take a crack at that question—about what it takes to generate public demand for a national resurgence—because I've had some pertinent experience along that line.

My experience had to do with trying to generate a consensus to support a grand escape attempt from a Hanoi prison. The parallel sounds farfetched, perhaps, but hang on; it will clear up. You might first ask: Why should generating support for an escape attempt be difficult? Everybody knows that the prisoner's code requires escape whenever possible and unanimous support of all escape efforts.

In fact, it was not until late—when we were approaching our sixth or seventh year in the lockup—that the ardor of some for a big breakout cooled. Over the years several groups had, after months of planning and preparation, made it over the wall and into the jungle—only to be recaptured, returned and tortured for names of collaborators in their effort. In time, the North Vietnamese imposed campwide reprisal actions following each escape. Bones were broken. The subject of escape became an emotional issue; to argue for more escapes, even when the way had been paved for better-than-ever chances of success, was to ask people to accept risks and to pay costs in support of an *idea*. The escape idea is a good idea, a heroic idea, but, for the guy who stays behind, as most of them must, it's just an abstraction about which the question, "What's in it for me?" has no answer.

What I'm saying is that asking for a public demand for an American resurgence in the name of that good and heroic idea of human freedom poses the same problem. You're asking people to accept risks and pay costs when their answer to "What's in it for us?" is necessarily unclear.

Here's the way arguments over "ideas" line up. You have, on the one side, the supporters of the heroic idea—call them romantics or idealists. You have opposing them the profit-and-loss guys, the bottom-line guys, the efficiency worshipers—the systems analysts, if you will. And then in the background you have the silent majority, or should I say tongue-tied majority, too proud to deny the validity of the idealists' arguments, yet too timid to lay their necks on the line.

How does the debate come out? On which side does the silent majority throw its weight? It depends on the frame of reference within which the argument is conducted. If the bottom-line guys, the accommodators, are in control, most escape plans will be scrapped. Fellow prisoner John Dramesi wrote a book about his Hanoi escape plan's being scrapped because the criterion for go/no-go was the straight-sounding, bottom-line test: "Compare what we all have to gain with success to what we all have to lose with failure."

Well, no escape could ever go with that criterion, with that rule of evidence. If such a test had been the standard of judgment of the U.S. Navy in 1942, Admiral Spruance would never have engaged the Japanese fleet at the Battle of Midway, and we might have lost World War II. Of course, World War II was fought before the systems-analyst cult had gained the upper hand and imposed such clamps on inspired action. Dramesi's book, *Code of Honor*, covers territory familiar to me because, as you can read, I was the leader of the romantics who tried unsuccessfully to carry out his plan. All was poised in readiness that March morning in 1972 when a faint-hearted colonel pushed two years' work down the drain.

Dramesi's book is well named because, as I saw it, it was in fact *honor* that was in the balance. On the other side of the scale was a profit/loss ratio, a "What's in it for us?" measurement. American resurgence in the name of freedom is in the same predicament as is honor in a "What's in it for us?" test. Any idea is in trouble if a group opposing it, an in-group, is allowed to set up the criteria which evidence supporting it must meet.

The issue of national defense policy should not be the private property of this or that cult and its particular definitions of reason or justice. To him who says that honor, being unquantifiable, deserves only a footnote in a rational solution, I can reply that sanctifying efficiency, for all its quantifiableness, is merely an expedient to avoid facing an important obligation, to avoid risk and pain.

The outcomes of our most important debates on national defense policy depend primarily on the biases (whether toward honor or toward efficiency, toward idealism or toward accommodation) of those who control the rules of admissibility of evidence, those who set the frame of reference into which the arguments must be hammered. It's obvious by now that I'm tired of being told that national policy decisions must be restricted to a bottom-line process, and that honor and idealism have to be checked at the door. I think that's wrong from a moral standpoint, and it's particularly wrong now if we are to keep the public ethos and public policy out of conflict. On issues pertaining to national survival, we don't have to accept narrow rules of evidence set by a self-serving cult which is at the same time tone-deaf to public sentiment. Transforming leaders, not myopic managers, should position the fulcrum for these arguments. The choice is both arbitrary and important. Remember Archimedes's lever; depending on where you put the fulcrum, either side can cause the world to move.

During Syb's and my delightful stay at the old Virginia, all-male, liberal arts college of Hampden Sydney, I wrote several more op-ed pieces for The Washington Post. *This one appeared on Sunday morning, January 25, 1981, the day our Iran hostages returned to America.*

THE HOSTAGES AS "EXTORTIONIST THEATER"

The Washington Post, January 25, 1981

As an eight year beleaguered and bludgeoned captive of Hanoi who spent most of that time in solitary confinement, I have in recent months been bombarding audiences from the eastern seaboard to Ohio to California with the message that America has been inviting future hostage disasters by so naively providing both actors and audiences in support of the new worldwide art form, "Extortionist Theater"—most recently successfully produced by Iran. Every outlaw power and terrorist group in the world surely took note of how Jimmy Carter's queasiness about the threat or use of force, and our national demand for continuous TV hostage soap opera, provided the positive and negative terminals of a power source into which they could plug a few American captives for profit and prestige. On my road show, I contrasted the Carter administration's assumptions about the basic nature of the captivity problem with the reality I knew behind barbed wire and proceeded to tear them apart. The samples below will give you an idea of what I mean.

False Assumption No. 1: "We must not hammer the captors or they'll take it out on the captives." Ask any of the 400 Americans in the prisoner's organization in Hanoi and they'll tell you that our North Vietnamese jailers were never more sweet than right after Col. Bull Simon's Son Tay helicopter rescue attempt (when he shot up a couple hundred of them, and they in turn, for security reasons, felt obliged to bring us leaders out of solitary and put all prisoners together in better living conditions in the big prison downtown), or during the B-52 bombings in December 1972 (when formerly abusive guards dropped their posturing and meekly broke precedent by bringing us tubs of hot coffee each dawn). Our bones got broken as often as not during America's sporadic bombing pauses when we were showing national "good will." Does the Iranian experience correlate with this? I think it does. Being nice to the enemy so he'll be nice to your captives is still a bush-league idea.

False Assumption No. 2: "We as a country are doing best by the captives if we support the infusion of 'a little bit of home' into their lives by sending visitors, at least during the Christmas season." Rev. Do-Good, or even William Sloane Coffin and Ramsey Clark, some Americans believe, are better than nobody. To fully realize the evil these people do, the damage they wreak on the morale and self-respect of the captives, one has to appreciate the tremendous ennobling and uplifting effect the overcoming of shared hardships has on a band of prisoners over time. In Hanoi, the greater the degradation and torture and the more years we withstood this together, the deeper grew the bonds of mutual respect and love for each other. Our world literally became our band of brothers, and personal pride and reputation among our peers, our total life's investment. Captors became symbols of tinhorn fakery.

Imagine now the stage of Extortion Theater onto which enter the friendly representatives of the people back home—all of whom are necessarily admitted as supplicants, as apologists. Moreover, these visitors are psychologically committed to dragging the captives before cameras as actors in the supplicant role. "Let the people at home see you" or "the intelligence people want to see you," they probably say. Though feeling humiliation, few captives can muster the emotional energy to take on these American finks as enemies. Each has enough enemies to concentrate on, even though these so-called friends are on the make, and they destabilize and damage the prisoner's life. Sometimes these finks damage his most prized possession: his reputation. Ramsey Clark came to Hanoi and incited American prisoners of war to violate their Code of Conduct and got a few takers. When does he account for that and for the disinformation he spread about the situation in Iran?

False Assumption No. 3: "Any release is a good release; if they'll agree to return 5 out of 52 next week, encourage it." Thank goodness this is often identified as a poor bargaining idea as seen from Washington; what our politicians and countrymen in general need to understand is the true and total perniciousness of early releases as seen from within that band of brothers behind barbed wire. Each person who walks out ahead of the others leaves behind him a trail of lifelong grudges and broken unity, and he installs within himself a time bomb of depressive remorse.

The early release idea also has the potential of providing the producers of Extortionist Theater with a grand finale act featuring the captives scrambling for places in line to go home by scoring high in an anti-American propaganda production contest. Hanoi had something like that in mind for us POWs, but I and others finessed that finale with strict orders to all Americans that there would be no exception to the Code of Conduct's prohibition against accepting parole. I also outlawed the accepting of amnesty. After our release, my constituents demanded justice in the form of prosecution of the few who bugged out in violation of my orders. Funny thing, though: I couldn't find anybody in Washington who understood the problem.

These problems and a dozen more like them need to be understood if we are going to truly shut down Extortionist Theater on a "never again" basis. This country has to get itself in hand, get its actors off the stage and get our audiences ready to shed not tears but rotten eggs and at least a credible threat of bombs and bayonets the minute the next bunch of punks tries to pull our chain by taking prisoners.

☆

Another op-ed piece of the winter of 1981. This was in connection with a then-ongoing and much publicized trial of an ex-POW.

WHAT NOT TO CONCLUDE FROM THE GARWOOD CASE

The Washington Post, February 9, 1981

I, like *The Washington Post*'s editorial of February 7, hope that America will salvage from the tragic case of Pfc. Robert A. Garwood both a clear definition of the standard of conduct to be demanded of any future POWs and an explanation of why a couple of career officers, accused of similar offenses, were not brought to trial. Also like the editorial, I have no enthusiasm for gloating over the downfall of one who "appears to be a born loser"; and I have a good track record for compassion behind bars. In fact, I took heat from some good men among the 400 in the prisons of Hanoi for what they considered my overgenerous offers of reinstatement and absolution of the very few "losers" (including those two career officers "who were not brought to trial") who would not conform to the minimum standards of our military organization. "It is neither American nor Christian to nag a repentant sinner to his grave," my words, were memorized by all as part of the law of the prisons. This piece is not about Robert Garwood's fate, but about the dead-wrong conclusions that are apt to be drawn from his episodes.

The first dead-wrong conclusion falls out of the misleading metaphors that are liberally sprinkled throughout most of all modern journalistic writings on imprisonment. They keynoted the editorial of February 7, too: "brainwashed," "broken," "unable to understand criminality," etc. Before I am misunderstood, let me assure the reader that I am *not* trying to criticize low thresholds of pain or trauma-induced emotional instability or least of all to reflect credit on myself or my gung-ho friends. I am saying that "brainwashed" and "broken" are unfortunate metaphors because they imply that a third force, an unseen hand, somehow enters the jailer/prisoner picture and changes the character or predilections of the latter. I understand pain, isola-

---

tion, and degradation; I've had a lot of all three, and I have cried "I submit" and done what these punishments were imposed to get me to do more times than I'd like to admit. But there was no third force, no unseen hand, that absolved me of guilt. Americans came back to cellblocks in Hanoi after terrible tortures, sometimes literally years of isolation, haggard and despondent souls. But as soon as the home-comer's cell door was closed and the coast was clear, he tapped to his old friend next door, sometimes crying for joy at being back with his gang and told him what he had done. Both parties knew the territory too well to try to kid one another, and the guy just out of the meat grinder got what he deserved: compassion and forgiveness. To try to claim brainwashing or breaking would never do. It just doesn't happen that way.

Whenever this subject is raised, one sooner or later has to take on the psychiatrists. I've solicited the views of a number of these professionals on the subject of brainwashing. They're all over the board on it; I think I could find three to agree on most anything. When forced to argue the point on their turf, I quote my own psychiatrists. One in particular, a professor at a leading medical school, called on me last week. I think we agreed: consciousness can be diverted, the pattern of judgment can be disturbed, but a long-term character change is not in the extortionist's cards.

The last statement is important because prisoner misconduct charges of the sort I've seen over the recent years do not pertain to pain thresholds, depression or isolation, interrupted consciousness, discontinuities of judgment patterns or temporary factors of any sort. The charges are about character. Furthermore, there is insurance against temporary factors leading to conviction in the requirement for proof of intent in these matters.

Robert Garwood's is a particularly sad case, but to conclude from it that one's responsibility for long-term actions can be absolved by some sort of hypnotic whammy put on by an enemy interrogator or that our government should require lower minimum standards of conduct in prisons from those with disadvantaged childhoods would be dead wrong. I just can't place myself in prison and make those ideas ring true.

Equitability of treatment is a different story. In the dialogues *Apology* and *Crito*, which record Socrates' words when he is on trial for his life and later in prison awaiting execution, the founder of Western philosophy makes the point that the same standards of moral judgment should pertain whether one is under pressure or not. If one can personify a government and contrast its actions at two points in time, even when under different administrations, is it too much to ask that its legal philosophy should be consistent whether the country is under pressure from anti-war forces or not?

When we Vietnam War prisoners came home, a no-recriminations policy was announced by our government. Sounds good, right? There of course was a footnote that the court-martial systems would, as always, be available to prisoner-versus-prisoner, individual-versus-individual, legal charges that could be supported by evidence. As senior officer of the Naval Service, and a leader of prisoners in Hanoi, I soon realized that I had just inherited a bomb. The same kind of conscience and sense of responsibility that had motivated 98 percent of us in Hanoi over the years flowed in exactly the same direction it had in Hanoi, to the very point it should have flowed—to the boss—to me. My constituency rightly said: "You put out the word. We obeyed, we resisted being manipulated by the enemy, two officers flouted your orders, now you make justice serve."

Goodbye rest and relaxation, goodbye emotional quietude, hello nine months of hell as all the legal and investigative machinery of the Navy Department droned on under my daily monitoring as I, a supposed individual, bringing personal charges into the legal limelight, did my duty as my constituency and I saw it. Like *The Post*'s editorial on February 7, we were worried about conduct standards in the *next* war. The charges started off at mutiny and worked down from there. They fell out of sworn depositions taken from scores of key men in that constituency I was so proud to have led. Then the charges hit the street; then my kids started bringing in armloads of hate-mail from our family mailbox as our hoped-for restful homecoming went on through its first summer.

The Secretary of the Navy asked the Judge Advocate General if the evidence supported the charges. "Yes," the JAG and his whole legal staff answered as one man. The Secretary ruled that a public trial would be detrimental to the lives and families of the scores of returned POWs who would be called to testify. I bought that; I needed a vacation after ten years and I was tired. The Secretary studied the evidence, gave letters of censure to the two senior officers and retired them on the spot.

That's the story on the seniors who never came to trial, those same ones I scarcely knew but had by the code of our prisoner organization, and my code, the just responsibility to formally investigate and charge.

Let us hope that the U.S. Government feels a little more sense of responsibility for seeing that justice is done after the next prisoner return, and files its own charges.

☆   ☆   ☆   ☆   ☆

Vice Admiral Stockdale, as Senior Naval Service officer among POWs in Hanoi, had disciplinary jurisdiction over all Marines and Navy personnel in North Vietnam. He had no jurisdiction over Pfc. Garwood, who was incarcerated in South Vietnam.

EARLY
HOOVER INSTITUTION
YEARS

IV. *In the spring of 1981, eight years after eight years of imprisonment, we were back in California, feeling comfortable and at home. All four of our sons were on their way to independent careers far to the east, and Syb and I took up residence on the Stanford Campus, just two blocks from the Hoover Tower. Four books were under contract, I was teaching at least one undergraduate course a year and producing a continuous flow of articles of the sort below.*

FIGHTING FOOLS, THINKING COWARDS? OUR MILITARY ENTICEMENT SYSTEM IGNORES HONOR, DUTY, COUNTRY _____

Los Angeles Times, September 29, 1981

The nation that will insist on drawing a broad line of demarcation between the fighting man and the thinking man is liable to find its fighting done by fools and its thinking done by cowards.

—*Sir William Francis Butler*

With the advent of the All Volunteer Force, the armed services entered into a high-rolling game of barter and exchange for the cream of this nation's youth, banking on the supposition that they could compete with the civilian job market in attracting and retaining the highest caliber talent. However, with the military recruitment process now underpinned by a marketplace business ethic, the true meaning of service somehow got left out of the equation.

That a program that relies on enticements such as choice of duty station, delayed entry, the promise of specialized training, educational credits, and higher salaries should automatically accrue those drives that have kept this nation free for the past 200 years, namely "duty, honor, and country," has never tracked. The businesslike style of our recruiting has affected the outlook and perspective of both potential recruits and those already serving; for many, time in the armed services is simply another job. The Madison Avenue mentality is aiming us toward that bifurcated society of fighting fools and thinking cowards.

Yet history has shown that mercenaries do not win wars or maintain deterrence: people committed to their country and bound by a common duty do. An injection of the nonquantifiable factors that encourage people to serve in the military is overdue, regardless of the future of the All Volunteer Force.

Why won't Uncle Sam's enticement system work? Because the application of rational business concepts to the profession of arms runs contrary to the nature of war; rejects the strong probability of future war; ignores the fact that people, not machines or computers, will win future wars; and disregards the historic promise of freedom on which this nation was founded. The clear and simple rational model never captures the scope of the human predicament. Alfred North Whitehead was right when he said, "There is a danger in clarity, the danger of overlooking the subtleties of truth."

Despite the Star Wars technology of our weapons systems, the next war will be won by people. Sure, they will have very sophisticated arms, computers and the like, but I'm confident that there will be many times when victory or defeat will rest on the ability of the commander on scene to lead, motivate and inspire. I came home from Hanoi after years of listening to sophisticated weaponry pop and crackle in the big world outside the prison, convinced that it is not lasers but bayonets that will determine the course of history for years to come. I fear that our frenetic efforts to man the services fail to recognize this possibility. What our military needs is men and women whose sense of duty overrides personal concerns, whose sense of honor allows them to make do with less, and whose sense of country transcends ethnic or family allegiance. Just how can these people be attracted to the military when service requires not only meeting standards far above those of the common citizenry but also long hours, frequent separation, financial hardship and little recognition?

—First, by telling it like it is. Make it clear that there is a very real possibility that there will be combat, perhaps in a foreign country with which we have no clear ties. People, civilian as well as military, may be wounded or killed. Prisoners will likely be isolated and tortured. Moreover, when the chips are down there can be no more carrot and stick—no enticements, no perquisites, no easy way to opt out. Our warriors must rely on themselves and their fellow Americans. Looking out for Number 1 loses its validity very quickly when everyone is looking over the precipice together.

—Second, by appealing to that better man or woman who lives inside every person. Low-order enticements are short term and cannot match the higher-order commitment to duty and country. Contemplation during my years in solitary confinement led me to conclude that a good life is one that accumulates high-quality memories. Can memories of comfort and workaday life, even a workaday life spiced with financial coups, compete with memories of bold strokes of service which one knows in his gut really mattered in the course of history? For what, in his old age, would one trade his lifetime memories of uplifting comradeship in times of shared danger? For what, in his old age, would one trade that flush of comfort in knowing that he has paid his dues as he listens to the band strike up the National Anthem?

—Third, by underscoring the historic roots of this nation's freedom. We've fought wars around the globe in freedom's name and have paid a terrible price for our most fundamental national belief. All must be clear on the fact that those in uniform may someday sacrifice their lives for this country and the freedom for which it stands.

The long-term health of our nation depends to a great extent on the ability of our armed forces. Those in uniform are the ones who guard the passes and protect the ramparts. Let's not stoop to marketplace tactics to man our ranks. We owe to those who will don American military uniforms the untainted pride of service to their nation and the respect of a thankful citizenry.

HOW WILL WE REMEMBER VIETNAM?

San Jose Mercury News, January 3, 1982

It is only now that honest historians are becoming able and willing to write about the Vietnam War objectively, without bowing to any of those widely disparate factions that saw the conflict as anything from a holy crusade to a mistake, to a crime, even a conspiracy.

The passage of time, and such Asian events as Vietnam's imprisonment of hundreds of thousands, its invasion of Cambodia, the Sovietization of U.S.-built harbor and airport complexes, all serve to contrast the reality of the war with the mirage-like, emotional accounts of propagandists of that time.

I approached Vietnam from a different angle than most. I am a professional warrior, a professional fighter pilot. Chivalry is not altogether dead in that world; the fair fight is still about the only way you can get the fighter pilot's job done. Moreover, for years as a Navy test pilot I had taken chances that were not much different from those in combat. People like me who live their lives with violent death at their right hands tend to become detached, doing their duty without a feeling of personal hatred for those little people on the ground.

But after I was shot down on a combat mission over North Vietnam my feelings changed. My leg was broken as I landed near a town. Civilians with

---

This article originally appeared under the title "The Most Important Lesson of Vietnam: Power of the Human Spirit." Reprinted by permission, The San Diego Union. Copyright 1982.

clubs began the process of beating me to death when North Vietnamese soldiers intervened and took me prisoner. I soon found that in North Vietnam, all captured pilots were stripped of their military rights and treated as war criminals.

Any guard could strike or manhandle any American officer. Certain guards were assigned to a special detail of torturing American pilots for military information or propaganda. This torture was both stylized and efficient. The prisoner was heavily slapped amid loud Vietnamese shouts as a mood of unrestrained vengeance was set. Then he was pushed to the floor in a sitting position as the torture guard bound his arms with ropes that could be infinitely tightened by jerks on their ends. The guard then bent the prisoner forward and stood on his back, jerking the arm bindings tighter as the victim's head was forced down between his feet by heel pressure on his neck.

The American had the power to extricate himself from the pain and claustrophobia only by signifying his willingness to supply the information demanded by crying, "I submit!" Nerve damage was often done to the victim's arms by this device.

My viewpoint of the Vietnam War was that Eisenhower's domino theory was probably valid: that if North Vietnam took over the south, a chain reaction could be expected to proceed to the southwest. I also knew that South Vietnam was not really like the western democracy our government tried to pretend it was. I knew there was a formidable framework of a Communist infrastructure in the south that would have to be burned out. I also knew how militantly doctrinaire and disciplined the North Vietnamese were. Putting all this together, I thought, during the war, after it, and still today, that Barry Goldwater had the only sensible outlook: either move quickly against Hanoi with repeated high impact non-nuke hammer blows from the air or forget it. Vietnam was no place for the Army.

So how do I classify the tragedy of Vietnam, if not a crusade, a mistake, a crime or a conspiracy? I classify it as a misguided experiment of the Harvard Business School crowd—the "whiz kids"—in achieving foreign policy objectives by so-called rational game theory, while ignoring the reality and obstinacy of human nature.

These were some of the policy lessons of Vietnam: You can't finesse human nature, human will, or human obstinacy, with economic game theory. And you should never let those who think you can, call the shots in a war!

The central strategy of the North Vietnamese prison system was extortion pressure—pressure to get us to contribute to what turned out to be their winning propaganda campaign beamed at the American man on the street, pressure to get us to inform on one another. These ideas were tied together as integral parts of the whole and were to be extracted by the imposition of loneliness, fear and guilt—fear of pain, guilt at having betrayed a fellow prisoner.

From this cauldron came some basic ideas and guidelines, to which we learned to cling. And the most important idea, as we strove to maintain our sanity, was this: *You are your brother's keeper.*

When you are alone and afraid and feel that your culture is slipping away, even though you are hanging onto your memories—memories of language, of poetry, of prayers, of mathematics and so on—hanging on with your fingernails as best you can, and in spite of all your efforts, still see the bottom of the barrel coming up to meet you, and realize how thin and fragile our veneer of culture is, you suddenly know the truth that we all can become *animals* when cast adrift and tormented for a mere matter of months. It is then that you you start having some very warm thoughts about the only life preserver within reach—that human mind, that human heart next door. You unabashedly tap to him that you love him when you know he's to be taken out for torture.

The question is sometimes asked of those who have been in high-stress situations for long periods: "What kept you going? What was your highest value?" My answer is: "The man next door."

Today, I thank God that this eight-year ordeal has ended—eight years without contact with our families, our parent country or its government in Washington. I thank God that most Americans in that prison compound in Hanoi had the courage, the self-respect, the straightforwardness, and the character to carry them through those dark days with honor. Yes, I thank God for that—for the power of the human spirit.

MILITARY ETHIC
IS NOT AT HOME WITH
BUSINESS VALUES

Fremont, California, Argus, May 21, 1982

The entrepreneurial system of values is inextricably tied up with successful management, company and personal profit, and rational self-interest. With these the military ethic is not at home. The soldier cannot adopt the methodology of business without adopting its language, its style, its tactics and ultimately its ethics.

Efficiency displaces honor as the greatest good. The military ethos is or should be one of duty, individual sacrifice and group dedication. The traditional virtues of the military calling are loyalty, obedience and courage. There may be lessons to be learned from the quarterly profit sheet of IBM or Textron, but these lessons should supplement, not submerge, military standards and values.

From firsthand experience in a war that I studied from both flak-encircled cockpit and bomb-encircled Hanoi, I can testify that the managerial spell wrought on the military bureaucracy has done injury that will be hard to repair. Our business-school-oriented elite tried to manipulate rather than fight the Vietnam War. It would be good news to report that by the end of the conflict the entrepreneurial bewitchment of the military mind was broken. But unfortunately the spell still holds.

The symbiotic relation in which military leadership and industrial management find themselves today has a long history. Some would argue that the relation began before World War II. Few would deny that American industrial production was a weighty factor in winning that war. But few also would deny that by the end of that conflict the American military leadership was already finding the embrace of the nation's industrial complex a little uncomfortably tight. In his Presidential farewell address, Dwight Eisenhower warned against the dangers that could emerge from a too tightly locked-in military-industrial complex. But the really damaging quantum jump in the business-military relationship from a moral point of view did not occur until 1961, when Defense Secretary Robert Strange McNamara and his Whiz Kids took over the Department of Defense and tried to run the Vietnam conflict as if it were the Ford Motor Company with a knock in the engine and an unfavorable balance sheet.

Damage continued after the Vietnam War wound down to its inglorious close. Careerism persisted, fitness and efficiency reports grew even more inflated, readiness data, under the pressure of a pervasive bureaucratic zero effect mentality, continued to be falsified, juniors were scandalized by the indecisiveness, weakness, and—in some cases—outright dishonesty of their superiors.

With the closing down of obligatory military service the armed forces lost the strength of a cross-section of the nation's youth. Now they must make do with the least qualified segment of the nation's young people. They have to deal with illiteracy, drug abuse and alcoholism as well as with an increasing rate of desertion and criminality. Thus vital energies that should go to improving military standards are inhibited at the start.

During my tenure as President of the Naval War College, I gave a course in philosophy and "ultimate situation" literature called Foundations of Moral Obligation. Together we read many good essays by authors ranging from

Aristotle to Jacques Monod. But of all the readings, none stimulated more discussion than Richard A. Gabriel's piece, "The Nature of Military Ethics," an essay that served the author as a preliminary sketch for his new book, *To Serve with Honor*. My students were officers in midcareer; they ranged in rank from lieutenant commander to captain in the Navy and from major to colonel in the Marines, Air Force and Army. Most were Vietnam veterans. Their nearly unanimous vote was that entrepreneurial standards and the military ethos are, as Gabriel claims, fundamentally opposed, and that the American military establishment has been invaded to its detriment by the standards and values of an efficiency-oriented ethic.

To those who claim that Gabriel's argument is one-sided and that his view of management versus military is absolutist, I would agree. But I would add that this world moves forward on the shoulders of one-sided people. It is those who say "but on the other hand" who bring up the rear—useful support personnel perhaps, but they are not in the vanguard. Gabriel himself does not claim that the entrepreneurial and military ethics stand glaring at each other from polar extremes. Rather, he tells us that there is a range, a spectrum of values along which the military ethic stands as much on one side of the midpoint as the managerial value-system stands on the other.

☆   ☆   ☆   ☆   ☆

The above is adapted from the introduction to *To Serve with Honor* by Richard A. Gabriel.

☆

The presidency of my Naval Academy class changes every five years, and I was stepping down after finishing my stint. I offered these reflections in Annapolis.

THIRTY-FIFTH REUNION, CLASS OF 1947: REMARKS OF THE CLASS PRESIDENT _____

U.S. Naval Academy Class Chapel Service, October 23, 1981

Here we are, another five years down the track, another five years during which an additional twenty-seven of our loyal classmates have died, "perished to add their point of light to our sky," as Ralph Waldo Emerson expressed it. Today is a time for us, the living, to again take stock—to take stock of where we came from, and of where we are. We must re-interpret the history of our class in the light of the present; it is our duty to do this every so often.

A week ago today in Bath, Maine, I gave the principal address at the launching of our Navy's newest frigate, the *Aubrey Fitch*. I was nominated to do so by his son, Jack, a man about our age. Many of the Fitch family were at the ceremony, and I thought I should cover some highlights of our old Superintendent's life. As luck would have it, his memoirs, six boxes of his personal papers, are held in the Hoover Archives in the same building where my office is. I recently spent three days reading them.

As time goes on we get new perspectives, and the papers of that battle-tested warrior who reported as our Superintendent at age 62 gave me still another perspective of where we came from, of who we were, we in this academy from 1943 to 1946.

Superintendents nowadays are young (the last three have been junior to us). They are currently picked as educators and motivators. What a change from those war-spent older men of that era we knew. Our graduation platform was loaded with Admirals in their mid-60s. As I went through the archive boxes I found Admiral Fitch's prepared introductory remarks for that ceremony. There were pencil scratches in his handwriting all over them.

About half of what his Flag Secretary had carefully put down was scratched out. "Jakie" Fitch, as his classmates always knew him, had scrawled "three minutes" across the top, and had underlined it three times. He did leave the first sentence in. It read: "As a class, you have been given certain responsibilities that no previous class has had." Right after that he had etched a great big question mark and circled it.

Maybe his ideas of responsibilities were sort of off our scale on that June 5th, 1946. Just four years before that, it had been he who had tapped the Captain of the *Lexington* on the shoulder and matter-of-factly said, "Fred, it's time to get the men off this thing." Jakie Fitch was right. They did, and she blew up shortly thereafter. Twenty-seven hundred lives had been saved on that one judgment call alone.

In his papers can be found other responsibilities of magnitude. He had been what might be called the Chairman of the Honor Committee of the class of '06. By that I mean he was that first classman who always acted as referee for the grudge fights (not in boxing gloves, but the hand gloves you wear when you're working out on the punching bags) that were *unofficially* held on personal challenges over honor in those days. By late November of his first class year, that is to say late November 1905, Midshipman 1/c Fitch was refereeing his 20th such fight of the year. A youngster (football player) had called a second classman (wrestler) some names for what he thought was a cheap disciplinary shot. The second classman elected to have it out in the clandestine ring; they were both varsity athletes and were really going to it. In the—get this—23rd round, the football player really connected and the wrestler went down for the count. In fact, he died in the hospital the next day. There was a SecNav investigation. Heads rolled.

That was a near thing for Jakie Fitch. He told the truth, and the Secretary liked that about him. He was a tough little guy from Michigan—champion boxer, footballer, gymnast, oarsman, quarter-miler. He kept his cool throughout the investigation; he was used to working near the edge; he graduated seventh from the bottom of his class.

Maybe that's why Admiral Nimitz, who gave the main speech as you will remember, and who Admiral Fitch used most of his three minutes to introduce, made the point—three times, no less (the speech is with Fitch's papers)—that those who stand low often do well in the Fleet.

As near as I could tell from three re-readings of that commencement speech, the main message Admiral Nimitz had for us was to guard our health. He cautioned us to protect it, particularly to protect it from worry.

Let's face it, there was just not much for that generation who came into the Navy under McKinley and Teddy Roosevelt—served in the Great White Fleet, WWI, and then *themselves* brought into being what was the conventional wisdom of that day's best possible solution to the human predicament, namely the winning of World War II—not much for them to say to the class of 1947 that spring. Some of those old guys probably found themselves humming that old ditty about spoiled and pampered pets of Uncle Sam.

I think that that fact, the *feeling* of that fact by us, had a great deal to do with our becoming such an achievement-oriented, pioneering class. I don't mean that either our seniors or we bore any misgivings at graduation. I don't mean we weren't happy at graduation. I mean that as we went to our first ships and met our whole generation and the one before it coming back the other direction, some of you besides me must have experienced what a Somerset Maugham character described as "the bitterness of an end achieved." Add that to a general class profile of lots of pre-academy college, in some of the best colleges in the country, and you get fireworks and production and diversification. It doesn't take a degree in psychology to realize why we set out to make our *own* lives, our own world, in the Navy and Marine Corps, and in public service, and in business and in the professions.

And we did. We've made our marks in board rooms, in pulpits, in classrooms and libraries, in the U.S. Senate, in the Cabinet, on ships' bridges and in airplane cockpits (count the stars!), yes and in the Oval Office itself, and in prison cells (and not all of us who spent time in cells were prisoners of war, either). As a class, if not always men of wisdom, at least seldom men of ignorance. I'd settle to be described on the average as the sort of "men of right opinion" Plato writes of in his dialogue *Symposium*. No empty heads, no hollow chests.

And we all carried something out of this place that has *mattered* over these 35 years (in addition to our charge at graduation to avoid worry). We carried out a sense of what it is to be a leader, a teacher, a path-finder. And in this chapel where we mustered every Sunday, I hasten to add, many of us picked up a lasting sense of our Creator. Sometime I'll write about the time that big face of Christ on the window behind me now popped out of nowhere into my mind at the very instant I thought my goose was cooked in Hanoi. And I'm not the sort who normally has religious experiences like that.

Classmates, wives, and widows, we and our departed pals have had lives worth living. We share a common heritage of which I am always proud.

I wrote this article at the request of the American Educator, *the professional journal of the American Federation of Teachers.*

THE PRINCIPLES OF LEADERSHIP _____

The American Educator, Winter 1981

In most educational institutions, leadership is addressed as a part of courses dealing with values, tradition, sociology, or management. In one sense, that is the way it must be, for leadership is not a true discipline. It has no body of distinctive literature, no recognized spokesmen or established authorities, and no unique assumptions. Yet, the importance of leadership in all sectors of our society has never been greater, and I believe that there are some teachable and learnable truths that underpin good leadership.

Several years ago I introduced a course at the Naval War College in Newport, Rhode Island, entitled "Foundations of Moral Obligation," which was designed for a group of successful midcareer military officers and civilian government executives of comparable responsibilities. It seemed to me that the mentality of our military leaders, indeed the mentality of the bulk of both military and civilian midlevel executives in the Pentagon, was becoming largely that of pedestrian functionaries. That is harmless enough as long as business as usual and bureaucratic procedure continue to be the order of the day. But my experience at sea, firsthand observations on the battle scene as the Vietnam War started, and revelations in prison camp drove home to me the fact that such a mind-set breeds disaster when the unexpected occurs, when it becomes necessary to steer an institution into uncharted waters. Moreover I believe that every factor that prompted me to originate this course is equally applicable to the civilian sector of our population. Throughout society, we need people who are bored with business as usual but who are also imaginative, educated, and eager to handle the unexpected.

The single most important foundation for any leadership course is history. That discipline gives perspective to the problems of the present and drives home the point that there is little new under the sun. Without familiarity with the yardstick of four thousand years of recorded history, busy people, particularly busy opportunists, have a tendency to view their dilemmas as unique and so unprecedented that they deserve to make exceptions to law, custom, or morality in their own favor to solve their problems. We can all think of several disastrous consequences of this short-sighted dodge within the last decade.

That our problems should be held against the light and wisdom of the past was a major premise of my course. Classic thinkers conceived disciplines and bodies of thought that mankind has used profitably over the centuries to solve problems. To ignore this fund of wisdom is the epitome of vanity.

Of course, on a day-to-day basis, some people get along well enough by leaving considerations about right actions to their intuition. In the highly structured bureaucratic environments so prevalent today there is a temptation to let personal standards go at that. The exponential rise in the flow of communication, particularly of the printed word within organizations—the directives, the programmatic blueprints, the acronyms and the ever-new buzzwords—tends to deaden the moral sensibilities of the best of us. Life on the treadmill gives one a false sense of security that values will be issued by the system whenever the need arises.

In the military, for example, the fortunes of war have a way of throwing commanders into new decision-making territory where there is no one to issue philosophic survival kits. This can be a shocking ballgame. The usual considerations of conformity and bureaucratic ass-covering are quickly replaced by new considerations. Can the orders that have been issued be obeyed, and is the issuer willing to carry them out himself in order to set an example? Is the leader willing to commit himself to the full consequences implicit in his policies? Is it possible that, as Winston Churchill once warned, the middle road could lead straight to disaster? Indeed, the twists of politics, economics, and social revolution might thrust leaders in all fields out on a similar limb with similar considerations. I think any leadership course should proceed from this angle.

Philosophy is an equally logical discipline from which to draw insights into leadership. In my view, the approach of using trendy psychological chitchat case-study sessions usually leaves the class in a welter of relativism. Current literature tells me that the social sciences have not outgrown the ideology of relativism, an egalitarianism of ideas which most philosophers have long since questioned. If one leads men into battle committed to the idea that each value judgment is as good as the next, he's in for trouble. Thus, the discipline founded by Socrates, that is, a discipline committed to the position that there is such a thing as central, objective truth and that what is "just" transcends self-interest, provides a sensible contrast to much of today's management and leadership literature. It is this philosophy and ultimate-situation literature that I recommend.

Included in the reading list for a leadership course, for example, could be Plato's *Dialogues*, Aristotle's *Nichomachean Ethics*, Immanuel Kant's *Fundamental Principles of the Metaphysics of Morals*, Arthur Koestler's *Darkness at Noon*, Herman Melville's *Billy Budd*, Albert Camus' *The Plague*, Joseph Conrad's *Typhoon*, and Stephen Crane's "The Open Boat."

One of the most productive results of my course was the development of a framework that focused on universal principles broad enough to handle most situations and specific enough to describe much of what the leaders will experience. This allows the teacher to draw on many different disciplines and fields of study—literature, history, art, science—to illustrate these principles. The level of instruction can be tailored to the students' needs, their familiarity with the material, and general academic acumen. Ten principles that I have listed below evolved during the several times that I taught the course and have come about as a result of study and experience rather than course planning. The fundamental presumption is that the student will eventually reach the same conclusions on his own without being pushed or manipulated. These principles, distilled from many sources, may come in an infinite number of variations, but I believe that they are valid under all conditions, in peace, war, behind the desk, in the heart of a corporation, or in the cockpit of a jet fighter.

Principle 1. You are your brother's keeper. In an environment in which people are trying to manipulate others—be it prison, a rigid hierarchical organization, or a bloated bureaucracy—there is always the temptation to better your own position by thinking only about yourself. Yet sooner or later, it becomes clear that the greater good for you and your fellow inmates, the key to happiness, self-respect, and survival, lies in submerging your individual instincts for self-preservation in the greater common demoninator of universal solidarity.

The opportunist may make significant short-term gains by walking over his fellow workers, by taking credit for their good work, or by superficial theatrics. But for each time he loses faith with his peers he forfeits some of his self-respect. As the nineteenth-century Swiss historian Jacob Burckhardt wrote, "Honor is often what remains after faith, love, and hope are lost." Hanging together, watching out for the other guy, can become a great source of strength.

Principle 2. Life is not fair. The existence of evil in the world has produced one of the oldest problems that humankind has pondered; man has had a most difficult time accommodating it. There is no moral economy in this universe in which virtue is rewarded and evil punished. To become unglued when you first discover this hardest lesson of life, and particularly when you are under pressure, is to flirt with danger. Life's silver lining is a creation of the optimist, and under pressure, the optimist is a hazard to navigation.

Today, the statement that life is not fair draws ridicule, but it is nevertheless true. For an interpretation of a good man's defeat I prefer the original poem of the Book of Job, the way it was before some ancient revisionist historian spliced on a happy ending. The story of Job goes a long way toward explaining the "Why me?" of failure. The story starts by establishing that Job was the most honorable of men. He then lost all his goods and his reputation. His wife badgered him to admit his sins, but he knew that he had made no errors. Here was a man who came to unexplained and unjustified grief without the solace of reason or logic. To handle tragedy may, indeed, be the mark of an educated man or woman, for one of the principal goals of education must be to prepare people for failure.

Principle 3. Duty comes before defiance. At his trial Socrates made the point that he owed it to Athens not to disillusion the citizens about its laws. If in doubt, he would defy the system only as an exception, only when he was positive it was evil. "I will never do what I know to be evil or shrink in fear from what I do not know to be good or evil," he said. A comparison of Socrates' approach to conscience in Plato's *Dialogues* with that of Thoreau in his essay *Civil Disobedience* is in order here.

Principle 4. Compulsion and free will can coexist. Aristotle laid down the law on this one. To say, "I spilled my guts because I was being tortured" is never an adequate explanation. To what degree were you incapacitated? How much information did you give? Whom else did you endanger by providing information? These questions must be answered. Aristotle would say the same to the man who says, "I stole the money because my kids were starving." More information is required before the act is justified.

Principle 5. Every man can be more than he is. Contrasting potentiality and act, Aristotle taught that every living thing strives to grow and flourish, aiming toward its particular end or good. Goethe once wrote that you limit a person's potential by appealing to what he is and that, rather, you must appeal to what he might be. Aristotle pointed out that persuasion is one of the primary responsibilities of any leader and categorized the methods of approach as appeal to reason (logos), appeal to emotion (pathos), and the appeal of the good character of the leader (ethos). Particularly in areas where there is no certain answer, ethos is the most persuasive.

Principle 6. Freedom and absolute equality are a trade-off. If you push individual freedom to the limit, you lose equality; if you subordinate every social value to equality, you lose freedom. The "leveling of America" type of equality contradicts our national, and even our Western, heritage. A growing ideology of relativism that tolerates, even honors, a lack of discrimination in thought has convinced too many people that they are good simply because they *are*. Their slogan, says author Lionel Trilling, is "Every man a Christ," the motto of what Tom Wolfe calls the me generation.

Principle 7. People do not like to be programmed. You can't force people to do what you think is good for them; you cannot persuade them to act in their own self-interest all of the time. A good leader appreciates contrariness.

Like the main character in Dostoevsky's *Notes from the Underground*, some men all of the time and all men some of the time knowingly will do what is clearly to their disadvantage if only because they do not like to be suffocated by carrot-and-stick coercion. "I will not be a piano key; I will not bow to the tyranny of reason." This is a plea that any good leader understands.

Principle 8. Living in harmonious ant heaps is contrary to man's nature. This is straight out of Solzhenitsyn's *One Day in the Life of Ivan Denisovitch* and Dostoevsky's story about the Grand Inquisitor from *The Brothers Karamazov*. Life makes sense only when the element of freedom is included in the mix.

Principle 9. The self-discipline of stoicism has everyday applications. The lessons in *Enchiridion* by the stoic philosopher Epictetus may come hard to the martini-drinking fighter pilot or the swinging executive with all the right contacts, but the Stoic's strong medicine is worth taking. Take it from one who knows how unexpectedly you can be trapped in a web of adversity, suffering, and cruelty, taken in an evil net, as the birds are caught in the snare, as the Biblical verse says.

Principle 10. Moral responsibility cannot be escaped. Whether you are a geneticist trying to unlock the secrets of life and its creation or a bureaucrat attempting to manipulate a nation's views of itself—pro or con—you cannot use your profession as a shield from responsibility for your actions. A person is the sum of his deeds, and the responsibility for them rests squarely on his own shoulders.

With these principles in mind, what, then, makes good leaders? First, we all need to be moralists—not posturers who exhort men to be good but thinkers who elucidate what is good. This requires first a clear idea of right and wrong and the integrity to stand behind your assessment of any situation.

Integrity is one of those words that many people keep in that desk drawer labeled "too hard." It is not a topic for the dinner table or the cocktail party. When supported with education, one's integrity can give him something to rely on when his perspective seems to blur, when rules and principles seem to waver, and when he is faced with hard choices of right and wrong. To urge people to develop it is not a statement of piety but of practical advice. Anyone who has lived in a severe extortion environment realizes that the most dangerous weapon of the adversary is his manipulation of his victim's shame. A clear conscience is one's only protection.

When we are down to the wire and the choices are limited, there is something in all of us that prefers to work with loyal, steadfast plodders rather than devious geniuses. A disciplined life will encourage a commitment to a personal code of conduct, and from good habits a strength of character and resolve will grow. This is the solid foundation by which good is made clear—by action and by example. A moralist can make conscious what lies unconscious among his followers, lifting them out of their everyday selves and into their better selves.

Also, there are times when our leaders must be jurists, when decisions will be based solely on their ideas of fairness, their knowledge of the people who will be affected, and their strength of character. There may be times when there won't be a textbook solution to go by. I'm not talking about petty legalistic arbitration or controls, but about hard decisions with seemingly endless complications. As jurists our leaders will be writing law, and that is a weighty responsibility. When they need the courage to withstand the inclination to duck a problem or hand it off, they must realize that it is necessary to take it head on. One note of caution, however: many laws necessarily will be unpopular, but they must never be unjust. Moreover, the leader must never write a law that cannot be obeyed. The job of a jurist is to guide others, not to put them in a Catch-22 position in which they are forced to choose between conflicting alternatives.

Our leaders will discover also that part of their duty will involve teaching. Every great leader I have known has been a great teacher, able to give those around him a sense of perspective and to set the moral, social, and motivational climate among his followers. This is not easy; it takes wisdom and discipline and requires both the sensitivity to perceive philosophic disarray in your charges and the knowledge of how to put things in order. A leader must aspire to a strength, compassion, and a conviction several octaves above that required by society in general.

Glib, cerebral, and detached people can get by in positions of authority until the pressure is on. But when the crunch develops, people cling to those they know they can trust—those who are not detached, but involved—and those who have consciences, who can repent, who do not dodge unpleasantness, and who can mete out punishment and look their charges in the eye as they do it. In difficult situations, the leader with the heart, not the soft heart, not the bleeding heart, but the Old Testament heart, the hard heart, comes into his own.

Another duty of a leader is to be a steward. This requires tending the flock—"washing their feet," as well as cracking the whip. It takes compassion to realize that all men are not of the same mold. Stewardship requires knowledge and character and heart to boost others and show them the way. Civil War historian Douglas Southall Freeman described his formula for stewardship when he said that you have to know your stuff, to be a man, and to take care of your men. In John Ruskin's words, such a process is "painful, continual, and difficult . . . to be done by kindness, by waiting, by warning, by precept, by praise, but above all, by example."

One final aspect of leadership is the frequent need to be a philosopher, able to understand and to explain the lack of moral economy in this universe. To say that is not to encourage resignation to fate but to acknowledge the need for forethought about how to cope with undeserved reverses. Just as the leader is expected to handle fear with courage, so also should we expect him to handle failure with emotional stability, or, Plato might say, with endurance of the soul. This is not to say a leader should be a good loser; what he needs is the ability to meet personal defeat without succumbing to emotional paralysis and withdrawal and without lashing out at scapegoats or inventing escapist solutions.

Humans seem to have an inborn need to believe that virtue will be rewarded and evil punished on this earth. When they come face to face with the fact that it is not so, they often take it hard and erratically. Faced with monstrous ingratitude from his children, King Lear found solace in insanity; the German people, swamped with merciless economic hardships, sought solace in Nazism. Aristotle had a name for the Greek drama about good men with a flaw who come to unjustified bad ends—tragedy. The control of tragedy in this sense is the job of the leader, indeed, the job of leadership education.

The only way I know to handle failure is to gain historical perspective, to think about those who have lived successfully with failure in our religious and classical past. A verse from the Book of Ecclesiastes says it well: "I returned and saw that the race is not always to the swift nor the battle to the strong, neither yet bread to the wise nor riches to men of understanding, nor favors to men of skill, but time and chance happeneth to them all." The test of our future leaders' merit may well not lie in hanging in there when the light at the end of the tunnel is expected but rather in their persistence and continued performance of duty when there is no possibility that the light will ever show up.

DIGNITY AND HONOR
IN VIETNAM

The Wall Street Journal, April 16, 1982 (Based on an Address before the Commonwealth Club of California, San Francisco, February 26, 1982)

Chivalry was dead in my prison. Its name was Hoa Lo, meaning "fiery furnace," located in downtown Hanoi, a prison the French built in 1895.

I arrived there, a prisoner of war in North Vietnam, in the late morning of a rainy Sunday in September 1965, a stretcher case. I had a broken leg (which my welcoming party, a street mob of civilians, had inflicted), a broken back (which I charge off to my carelessness in not having had the presence of mind to brace myself correctly before ejecting into low-altitude, high-speed air from a tumbling airplane), and a gunshot wound in my good leg (which an irate farmer had pumped into my stretcher during my first night on the ground, an act I credit as morally neutral just to keep the score balanced). The North Vietnamese officer who presided over my arrival after three days in the back of a truck was about my age (42 at the time), also a career military man.

I asked him for medical attention for my broken bones and open wounds. "You have a medical problem and you have a political problem," he said. "In this country we handle political problems first, and if they are satisfactorily resolved, that is, if you demonstrate a proper understanding of the American war of imperialist aggression in Vietnam and take concrete actions to stop it, we will attend to your medical problems." That was the last time the subject of medical attention for me ever came up in my next eight years as a prisoner of war.

In intense, bizarre form, the prison was an extortion factory, a propaganda factory. It was much like the one Dostoyevsky described in 19th Century Siberia, like the one Solzhenitsyn described in the modern Gulag. It was almost identical to the one Koestler described in the Moscow of the Stalinist purges, in that prison book, *Darkness at Noon*, fiction no less, that gives me more shudders of authenticity than any other in print. Cervantes experienced the same pressures for seven years in a Moslem political prison in Algiers, after he was captured in the battle of Lepanto over 400 years ago.

These prisons are all the same; the name of the game is to unstring their victims with fear and polarize them with guilt. There are always more rules than can practically be obeyed, always a tripwire system to snare you in a violation that the jailers can brand as moral turpitude—and there is always an escape valve, a way to make amends if you repent.

The tripwire in Hanoi was based on the "no communication" rule. As with all tripwires, the prisoner had a choice to make and he stood to lose either way. If he obeyed and did not communicate with his comrades, he accrued the conscience problems of betraying his fellows and at the same time sentenced himself to a desperate loneliness which would likely get to him after a year or two. If he communicated, and this was the only way to go for loyalty, for a feeling of self-worth, for dignity, he would periodically be caught and tortured under the charge of ingratitude for the "humane and lenient treatment" he was being given.

(Incidentally, communication grew to be a very refined, high-volume, high-speed, highly accurate though dangerous art. We used the same code Koestler's fictional Commissar N. S. Rubashov used during his Moscow trial and execution period in the late 1930s.)

By torture, I don't mean leg irons or handcuffs or isolation. We were always careful to remind ourselves that those were just inconveniences, not to panic. By torture we meant the intentional imposition of pain and claustrophobia over as short a time as necessary to get the victim to "submit."

In my experience this is best done by heavily slapping the prisoner, seating him on the brick floor, reeving his upper arms with ropes, and while standing barefoot on his back cinching up the elaborate bindings by jerks, pulling his shoulders together while stuffing his head down between his feet with the heel of your foot. Numb arms under contorted tension produce an excruciating pain and a gnawing but sure knowledge that a clock is ticking while your blood is stopped and that the longer you wait before submitting the longer useless arms will dangle at your sides (45 minutes of blood stoppage usually costs about six months of dangle). The claustrophobia also concentrates the mind wonderfully.

How long to submission for a good man? About 30 minutes. Why not hold your silence and die? You can't just will yourself dead and have it happen—especially in that position. Why not just give them what they want and be done with it? Reasons that come to mind include dignity, self-esteem, contempt for B-grade pageants. They can make you tell them most anything they know you know. The trick is, year in and year out, never to level with your captors, never let them really know what you know.

There are a lot of things you can't do with torture. Aristotle said that compulsion and free will can coexist, and he was right. Unlike our courts, spring-loaded to excuse any action to which the general term coercion is attached, prison societies get down into the messy details of degree of coercion and complicity before making judgments. The man about to undergo torture must have burned into his mind the fact that he can be hemmed in only within a very narrow window and that he need not volunteer information or "spill his guts."

How exactly to behave in the ropes, to make the torture team work for everything they get—the specific information, the personal concessions—to give no indication that you're short on courage yet supply a convincing submission before you've lost your mental skills, to minimize their net gain after you are let up and sat before the tape recorder, are all matters of dramatic art—a deadly dramatic art, which if revealed for what it is will assure your being reduced to a whimpering heap in minutes.

For all this, it obscures the fact that the extortion experience, even in a harsh political prison, is not a physical experience. It's an emotional experience.

I do not mean an experience like "getting brainwashed" or "breaking" or falling into the arms of your captor, smitten by "Stockholm Syndrome." Yes, over time, pain and isolation, a "persuasive interrogator" and lack of sleep can probably bring about discontinuities in the victim's decision-making patterns, but never a "whammy" that would go as deep as character change. Nobody who has had any extensive experience in captivity would have the guts to try to pass on succumbing to intolerable pain or even suffering a nervous breakdown as a case of being "brainwashed" or "breaking" or developing a "syndrome." Seasoned hostages see these terms for what they are—polite expressions that allow the inexperienced to feel more comfortable in avoiding the issue of holding a person responsible for his actions.

To keep your integrity, your dignity, your soul, you have to retain responsibility for your actions, to deal with guilt. ("Yes, I lost the bubble, I might have done better, but I didn't.") You need to look squarely at what you did and measure its limited gravity in the light of the overall truth of the total situation, then use the guilt, such as it is, as a cleansing fire to purge the fault, as a goad for future resolve, and above all not be consumed by it. But you have to do all this yourself. To say guilt doesn't exist or that it was the work of "evil spirits" or "brainwashers" is self-delusion.

The political prison experience is an emotional experience in that you learn that your naked, most inner self is in the spotlight, and that any detected shame or deep fear, any chink in your moral armor is a perfect opening for the manipulative crowbar. And once the manipulator gets it into you, he can put you out front working for him because he has something on you of which you are genuinely ashamed; he has the means to destroy your reputation if you fail him. Fates like that are what prison nightmares are made of, not fear of pain.

When good people try to commiserate with a person coming out of these circumstances, the language of both parties seems to find common meaning only in terms of physical things—years of solitary, months or years in leg irons, torture stories, mail deprivation, weight loss and so on. Relatively speaking, those are hardly problems at all. (It was not uncommon among us to try to starve yourself, to make yourself an immobile Gandhi, just to take yourself out of the eligibility zone of those they were trying to entrap into public exposure with the touring of a "fact-finding" American.) For us, the deprivations from the physical side of the good life and even the pain and the loneliness were shallow complaints compared to finding yourself stripped of all entitlement to reputation, love or honor at home.

I am often asked: "What are the attributes of those who best measure up in these circumstances?"

Rather than high thresholds of pain, I think it was the persistent practitioner of endurance who carried the day for courage. The game of physical intimidation was not won or lost in one grand showdown. The hero of us all was the plucky little guy who made them start all over every day, the person who refused to accept the extortionist's logic of "being reasonable," of accepting the inevitable, of granting yesterday's tortured concession free of charge today.

Fierce political dedication undoubtedly strengthened the resolve of some. But if I were an interrogator trying to make a good estimate as to whether the new prisoner across from me was likely to be a soft touch, I wouldn't base my estimate on the vehemence of his political protestations. But I would be delighted if he seemed to need my reaction to his expression of political virtue. The player who needs to interact with those around him, even his enemies if friends are not available, is an extortionist's dream. Lock people like that up for a few months and they start looking for a friend.

Religious conviction? It was certainly a positive force for the great majority of us. But indispensable? No. Some good prisoners did not rely on it. What is indispensable to avoiding entrapment in the web of fear and guilt is the ability to stand isolated, without friends and surrounded by entreaters, and quite uncharitably say "no," without embarrassment, with finality and with commitment to the consequences. This is a very hard thing for many well-brought-up, mannerly, considerate, American men and women to bring themselves to do. It seems so impolite to leave it at just "no."

This sort of thing was a big initial hurdle for the typical young, well-brought-up, well-educated American pilot in prison. He was put through the gauntlet when shot down, and maybe the next day's target list was beaten out of him. This he more or less expected. But a month later, after lying low, learning to communicate through the wall, receiving all the standing orders of unified resistance, he is pulled out for interrogation and told to read Harrison Salisbury's Hanoi articles from the *New York Times* over the prison public-address system. He has been warned by the American next door that this would be coming up. Moreover he has been coached by this experienced friend, and so he goes through the dialogue, but it seems awkward to him this first time:

"Good morning," says the interrogator. "You look well. I have your first assignment for you. We want to provide the American criminals with news from U.S. newspapers, but we Vietnamese have an accent that makes us difficult to understand on the camp radio. You will read these American articles into the tape recorder and they will be played at noon today."

"No."

"What do you mean, no. The camp regulations require that you obey all orders. You must do it. My superior has decreed that you shall do it."

"I refuse."

"You can't refuse. You must obey the laws of this country. You are a criminal. If you refuse, you will be severely punished. Shall I call the guard and have him punish you? I think you remember the punishment, and that you cannot overcome it. What do you say?"

"I say nothing. The problem is not mine, it is yours. It's up to you."

Many of us are brought up to believe that a person, particularly a person in authority, is entitled to an explanation, at least a better answer than a figurative "stick it in your ear." It seems so unfair, so unnatural not to drop in a word of regret or at least a counterproposal. (And any smart extortionist will know that.)

It was the counterproposal that our captors counted on to get us to the hook—we became partners that way, guilty partners. "You are an American, you are a pragmatist, your submission is inevitable. We don't like to punish you. Meet us half way. Be reasonable."

Americans in Hanoi learned fast. They made no deals. They learned that "meeting them half way" was the road to degradation. My hypothetical young prison mate soon learned that impulses, working against the grain, are very important in political prisons, that one learns to enjoy fighting city hall, to enjoy giving the enemy upside-down logic problems, that one soon finds himself taking his lumps with pride and not merely liking but loving that tapping guy next door, the man he never sees, the man he bares his soul to after each torture session, until he realizes he is thereby expiating all residual guilt. Then he realizes he can't be hurt and he can't be had as long as he tells the truth and clings to that forgiving band of brothers who are becoming his country, his family.

This is the power of comradeship and high-mindedness that ultimately springs up among people of good will under pressure in mutual danger. It is a source of power as old as man, one we forget in times of freedom, of affluence, of fearful pessimism—like now.

Eight years in a Hanoi prison, survival and dignity. What does it all come down to? It does not come down to coping or supplication or hatred or strength beyond the grasp of any normal person. It comes down to unselfish comradeship, and it comes down to pride, dignity, an enduring sense of self-worth and to that enigmatic mixture of conscience and egoism called personal honor.

COMMENCEMENT ADDRESS _____

St. John's College, Santa Fe, New Mexico, May 16, 1982

It is a matter of great pride on my part for me to be affiliated with St. John's College. I feel a strong kinship with the students here. The kinship I feel is from what I fancy to have been my own version of St. John's education. That began only in my late 30s with two years of graduate study in philosophy and politics at Stanford University, and was followed shortly thereafter by four years of solitary philosophic contemplation in a prison cell in preparation for my orals. I am finally meeting that appointment today.

Thus you and I, class of 1982, know what it's like to have a four-year "melting" experience under pressure. Yours has been a program that materialized before your very eyes as a one-way street, an irreversible process with no turning back, where even treading water was not feasible. And to swim you found you had to jettison your protective armaments, your prejudices, your posturings, just to stay afloat. It has been total immersion in a program that made the truth known to you that in the cauldron you must intellectually grow or intellectually die.

And the heck of it is, you can't even explain this demanding, inspiring, *extruding* experience you've just completed to the man on the street, including in particular your counterparts enmeshed in the mob scenes of big trendy campuses, campuses dedicated to supplying the world with technocrats and functionaries. To all too many men on the street, the classical curriculum here at St. John's gets translated as an excursion through the soft-headed social sciences, a misconception that I'm sure is as offensive to you as that man on the street's (*sympathetic* man on the street's) seeming inability to comprehend the true thrust, the direction of travel, of some of my more stressful, yet at one and the same time, enhancing melting experiences.

Perhaps what I'm saying is that I feel a kinship with St. John's students because we are both sympathetically regarded by audiences who don't know the half of it, in many cases audiences who don't know what critical thought and toughmindedness are all about.

I'm finding that one of the benefits of being a Visitor and Governor of St. John's College is receiving thoughtful letters from students, including a particularly nice one giving me insight into the class mood toward today's activities. He expressed the pride of achievement you all feel, and also the vague apprehension as you approach an uncertain world dominated by people who "don't know where you're coming from," as they say. Your classmate wrote that it was his hope that I would treat the latter difficulty with a note of realistic optimism.

So my plan is to do that, to give you some information that I hope you will accept as realistic optimism. And I'll close with a poetic suggestion as to how a St. Johnnie might best look at the man on the street problem.

Now for the information. While driving over in the car from Colorado Springs this morning my wife, Sybil, asked me, "What are you going to talk about?"

"Human nature," I replied. She laughed out loud. Now it's your turn to laugh because I'm really presuming to give you some information about that most open-ended of all subjects. That sounds both presumptuous and naive, doesn't it?

Think of it this way. Think of a big laboratory experiment. It is a very expensive experiment, so expensive that even here in America we couldn't afford it. The reason is that the subjects are humans and it takes about 50 of them full time, 24 hours a day, for four years. Now these subjects will be very healthy, college-educated men in their 20s, 30s (some of us even our 40s). Each will be sealed individually in a box ten feet long and four feet wide. They will be prevented from seeing each other throughout the four-year period. They will have no pencil, no paper, no books. They must live in absolute silence. They will be traumatized or crystallized with an outside threat, and I, as an insider, will take mental notes of what makes them tick. During this four years I will select out five or six general traits, traits that are rather different than you might expect. Now after this experiment, if what I report isn't "information about human nature," what is it? Moreover, such data has never been recorded before.

Notice that I presume you here at St. John's think there is such a thing as human nature. Some intellectual groups are trying to write it off, you know. It is too troublesome a thing to work into their social architecture for the future. I met some highly placed intellectuals like that at a recent curriculum-planning conference on how to educate leaders for the 21st century. They said, "Wow, in the 21st century, all previous bets are off!" "It's a completely new ballgame." "The world of individuality and ego has got to go; we've got to erase these outmoded bad habits of several thousand years and get everybody situated in antheaps." "Put away that curriculum you brought, Stockdale, that reading list with all those old books." "No more old books!"

I don't see how you could go through the St. John's curriculum and not conclude that the mutation of human characteristics proceeds, at its very fastest, with glacier-like leisureliness. That's clear even in the reading I do. For instance, I feel that in my lifetime I've personally known half the characters Homer described in The Iliad three thousand years ago. Hector is about to leave the gates of Troy to fight Achilles. He will lose and he will die. When he says goodbye to his wife and baby son by the gate, the baby becomes frightened by the nodding (you can't beat Homer for descriptive figures of speech) of the plumes on his father's shining helmet bobbing in the breeze. You have it all in that instantaneous snapshot: Hector's duty, his wife's tragedy, Troy's necessity, the baby's cry. That's almost a picture of my family in the 20th century.

Jeffrey Hart gave me the idea for that example above. He is an English professor at Dartmouth. He complains that many of his students up there don't know where they come from. He also says that in a classical sense, a citizen should be a person who could, if necessary, re-found his civilization. That's what was necessary, and happened, in that grand experiment I'm going to recount. A civilization was re-founded by people stripped to the core, stripped of all the accoutrements of their former society.

What came through those walls, tapped in code from box to box in this sort of state of nature circumstance? Nastiness? Dogmatism? Bitterness? Saintliness? Reasonableness? Joyfulness?

The answer has to be, "Some of all of the above, from time to time," but the human characteristics I'm digging for lie beneath issue-oriented fallouts, and I hope even beneath attitudes.

At that depth, what did I find? (I'm going to concentrate on the very interesting and surprising.) I found people who were: *ritualistic, poetic, fascinated* by *astronomy, numbers,* and *music* (the seven liberal arts were not pulled out of a hat, after all), *highminded, private.*

I'm trying not to tell this as a prison story, but in passing, I want to mention that the very best was written by Arthur Koestler in about 1940. The title you recognize, I'm sure, *Darkness at Noon.* The book, about the final imprisonment and execution of an old Bolshevik founding father during the Stalinist purges of the late '30s, is fiction but it raises on my brow more cold sweats of memory, of authenticity, than any of its less perceptive autobiographical counterparts. Like the midwest cornfields I grew up in, the plots and cross-plots track in flawless rows up and down, straight across, and diagonally. I'm going to talk about just one exchange in that great book and it is an exchange that haunts me. It has to do with two strains of human virtue. One epitomizes the cry from today's pulpits: "Don't just sit there and pray; get out and *do* something to better the world!" And the other says, "Pray for your own decency and save your own soul."

It goes like this. Old Commissar Rubashov is brought back to his cell after a long interrogation by a ruthless upstart named Gletkin who has undertaken to instruct his elder in goodness and honor. The old man is starting to give ground under the forces of fatigue and extortion and muses to himself about Gletkin's final admonition: "Honor is nothing more than being useful to others." This utilitarian view is commonly heard in many quarters, and is certainly one we would expect from a Marxist but by no means only from Marxists. But there is something about it that worries the old fellow, and he checks the shadows and the sounds and ascertains, as any old prisoner will, that there is no guard waiting silently to pounce at his first detection of wall-tap sounds. And he taps—literally "talks"—in the same monotonal code we used in Hanoi, in the same code the second century Greek historian Polybius wrote of. "What do you think of honor being defined as simply being useful to others?" he asks his next-door neighbor, a slightly eccentric Czarist aristocrat who has not been out of his cell for ten years. "Honor is decency. It has nothing to do with usefulness," is the blunt reply.

What I saw had more to do with decency than utility.

Trait 1: Ritualism. Once a human being is isolated in silence, seeing only one face twice a day, the face of a man who does not speak his language and delivers a bowl of rice, he thinks it's merely a matter of time till he goes crazy. No such luck. After a couple of months you realize you're stuck with yourself and you might as well get used to it. Sometime soon after that it seems to occur, even to the sort of person whose college room was always chaotically disorganized, that you've got to get some routine into your life or you're going to become an animal. Each in his own way seems to set time aside for exercise, for meditation, and of course for communication with that neighbor next door at that time of day when the chances of being apprehended are least. One senses that it's "get organized or die." The day becomes full. I can remember saying to myself, "It's late afternoon and the guard is coming with the leg irons for the night and I haven't had a minute to myself. Time flies. Where has the day gone?"

Trait 2: Love of poetry. Another surprise. When your mind gets dried out, as the silence of months overtakes you, you thirst for things to remember. The clutter of all the trivia evaporates from your consciousness and with care you can make deep excursions into past recollections—bringing up seating arrangements at age five birthday parties and the like. Of course you learn how not to jolt your memory and derail it, you know how to quit digging when you're tightening up, to relax and think of something else and know the missing link will pop out at you in due course. It's then that the love and memorization of poetry becomes an almost universal preoccupation. Verses were hoarded and gone over each day. Many were composed and sent along for criticism. But the person who came into this experiment with reams of already memorized poetry was the bearer of great gifts. I often chuckled to myself about the professor I had who used to say "Never waste your time memorizing anything you can look up in the library." If we had all followed advice like that, our civilization would have been a very barren thing.

Trait 3: Love of those liberal arts Astronomy, Numbers and Music. Everybody seemed to know what date it was all the time. There is nothing to that old tale about the prisoner who puts an "x" on the wall every day (also you wouldn't dare put "x's" on walls in Hanoi). There was lots of discussion about the vernal equinox and the phase of the moon because unlike dates, Easter was a more involved day to identify. Anyone so fortunate as to catch sight of the moon was obliged to describe its exact phase. In the dust of the cell floors, almost everybody had at one time or another spent that wonderfully interesting month or so figuring out, in view of the way the earth went around the sun and the moon went around the earth, just exactly how the shadows of the earth should be reflected as moon phases.

When it came to numbers I was very fortunate to have a friend who had a master's degree in math who would pass me the sort of expansions found in the back of engineering manuals. One was precious—it was the one in which "e" to the "x" is equal to the sum, from "n" equals 1, to "n" equals infinity, of the expression "x" to the "n minus one" over "n minus one" factorially. Shortly after he gave it to me I was banished to an area where there were no Americans to tap to for a whole winter and spring. I became the world's greatest authority on the exponential curve. That formula allowed me to figure natural logarithms to three or four decimal places in five or six iterations with a stick in the dirt. By scratching them into the bottom of a bedboard with a nail I luckily found, I established tables, converted to the base ten, went through all the scales of the slide rule, and became one of the very few people on earth to actually know why any number to the zero power is necessarily one, why zero factorially is necessarily one. (What a pity today's computer-age kids miss the symmetry of the exponential system.)

A year later I was lucky enough to be returned to the immediate vicinity of my mathematical friend. We both had played the piano, and our cross-courtyard under-door finger signaling fell into the subject of musical scales, why you can't have both seven sharps and seven flats, and how scales that sound good to us have unsymmetrical frequency distributions. We discussed the peculiarity of the latter. How can that be? Is what sounds good a cultural accommodation without regard to mathematical symmetry? Is that why oriental music sounds funny? Of course it became obvious to us (after several months of contemplation) that there had to be a particular proportionality constantly relating the frequencies of adjacent keys all across the piano keyboard (black to white, white to white, and so on). What was that particular constant? My friend went off the air for a day or two and just thought about it. He came back and said, "It has to be the twelfth root of two." In a few minutes (I had memorized my log tables), I ran that out to be 1.0591. When we got home a music teacher told me that he was right—that that twelfth root of two was a very important constant in music—it was even named after the genius who derived it in the 19th century, Helmholtz's Constant. My mathematical prison friend now has his Ph.D., but for some odd reason was not honored by getting his name hyphenated with Helmholtz.

Trait 4: Highmindedness. By this I don't mean "joyfulness," and I particularly don't mean "optimistic" (Viktor Frankl and I agree that babbling optimists are the bane of existence to one under stress—give us a pessimist every time for the long pull). What I mean is the gradual erosion of natural selfishness among people of good will facing a common danger over time. The more intense the common danger, the quicker the natural selfishness melts. In our situation, at about the two-year point, I think most of us were thinking of that faceless friend next door, that sole contact with our civilization, that lovely complicated imaginative human thing we had never seen, in terms of "love" in the highest sense. By later comparing notes with others I found I was not alone in getting so noble and righteous that I could hardly stand myself. People would willingly absorb physical punishment rather than let it fall to their friends. Questions arose in my mind about the validity of the much talked about instinct of self-preservation.

I've since done a lot of reading about this, and this phenomenon has lots of precedent, from battlefields and elsewhere. Those who wring their hands at frightful prospects in these "ominous times," apparently don't know it, but the human spirit has a lot of nobility that doesn't show till the going gets tough. You don't have to develop this asset. It will rise, as it has throughout history, to meet great challenges.

A kind of corollary to this highmindedness came to mind as I was having lunch one day last week at the faculty club at Stanford with a classics professor. We just had a chance meeting, neither of us had a reservation, and we sat side by side at a general members table. In talking about improving the human condition he offered the suggestion that a good first cut would be to maximize individual autonomy. That suggestion, as I told him, would not pass the test of my experiences under pressure. Those who led their juniors in our situation by saying something like, "This is a difficult and complicated environment, and I leave it to each one of you to pick your own course and do what you think best," rapidly learned that human beings under pressure will not tolerate such a cop-out. It sounds good, and if the pressure is light they'll hold their fire of outrage for a long time, but ultimately and particularly when the pressure is heavy, they'll say, "You have no right to avoid personal responsibility like that." "I deserve to live in a predictable society where I can count on an established consensus of right and wrong." "To sententiously just urge us to do the good in a situation like this is phony; you owe it to us to *tell us what the good is*." "We must have law. It is your duty to write it; and it is your duty to stand responsible for the consequences of it."

It's difficult to explain this highmindedness that sets in when you're down the trail a way. Solzhenitsyn says it well in one of his Gulag writings:

> It was only when I lay there on the rotting prison straw that I sensed within me the first stirrings of good. Gradually it was disclosed to me that the line separating good and evil passes not through states nor between classes nor between political parties but right through every human heart . . . and that is why I turn back to the years of my imprisonment and say, sometimes to the astonishment for those about me, "Thank you, prison, for having been in my life."

Trait 5: Privacy. I've described a very intimate relationship between next-door neighbors who know each other only by sound or fingertip motion, by "feel" in the sense that either mode can be made to imprint humor, sarcasm, grief, joy, all the emotions. But sooner or later we all had the experience of a fit of exuberance at suddenly "putting the universe together" in our individual hearts and minds, and of trying to relay these wonderful religious or at least generally inspirational keys to the kingdom next door. A very polite and tentative wall touch in reply usually told us "thanks a lot but no thanks." A supressed irritation was there and it was clear that what was meant was "I know you're performing an act of love, but you're getting into my private territory." "That solar plexus of my soul is mine alone."

It's my belief that part of being a human is to have a right to certain sacred turf and that he who would rob you of that privacy is violating your right to dignity, your right to selfhood. There are deep Western roots to this idea from the Aristotelian and Stoic sides: the notion of sovereignty over one's inner self which he alone controls. Fallouts include the Christian doctrine of personal responsibility for the saving of one's own soul, the English Common Law property right of a man's home being his castle and so on. Of course the experimental group's outside threat was from the extortionist, and although there are lots of ways of describing harsh extortion in terms of physical coercion and isolation, these are merely accelerators for the basic weapons of extortionists from ancient times: the imposition of feelings of fear and guilt in their victims. And that is done first by violating that self-hood, that human right, by getting the person to bare his breast, to expose his sacred turf, to "level," to "interact," to confess—and then to pack the wound with the rock salts of fear and guilt and catch your victim as he falls into your arms.

A political prison is just a worst-case vantage point from which to watch the obvious practice of this ancient art. On the more subtle plane, facilitators use it, religions use it, encounter groups live on it, demagogues preach it ("The end of the world is coming [fear]; give away your wealth [guilt]"), and of course it is formalized in communist dogma as the process of criticism/self-criticism. And the sad part is that I hear that some American businesses are starting to "motivate" their executives with these indecent exposures, these heart to heart sessions. Perhaps I overkill this today, but an old political jailbird senses that point when rational discourse ends and dirty tricks begin. He never forgets the pattern, never forgets the critical mix, and never loses the impulse to spike the action right at the changeover point.

The hero of selfhood is our friend, and in particular our President Delattre's friend, Sir Thomas More, the great legal mind of 16th century England. It is his case that best makes it clear that I'm not talking of secrecy or the protecting of deviousness. That gentle, reasonable, supple, humorous, unassuming and sophisticated man guarded his private turf of selfhood unto death, even against the pleadings of those who had initially backed him, for instance, his wife. He would not offend his human right to conscience and dignity by scribbling on a piece of paper a justification for Henry VIII's divorce, something which crossed a transcendental line with him. He chose instead to be beheaded in the Tower of London.

I let his example stand as the basis of my reasonable optimism for the future of this class of 1982. Nothing could spawn greater optimism than the confidence that there are courageous people about us who will occasionally remember feeling the authentic impact of genius at a St. John's seminar and know what is to take a stand on principle and guard the passes of our culture. Both subject matter and system here have focused on you graduates having a true knowledge of where you came from, and on helping you locate your "selfs" on the map—maybe even as Sir Thomas More, who "knew where he began and where he left off, knew what area of himself he could yield to the encroachments of his enemies, and what area of himself he could yield to the encroachments of those he loved."

Now for the poetic suggestion as to how to handle the man on the street problem. It's actually the suggestion of a classically educated Englishman,

Louis MacNeice. Louis MacNeice, now dead, started publishing poetry in 1925. He was head of programming (and of World War II anti-Nazi propaganda) for BBC. Like my philosopher professor who introduced me to him 20 years ago, I consider him a sensitive observer of the intellectual scene. I'll read parts of a long poem he wrote in the autumn of 1938, about the ominous world scene that fall, about his disappointment with Munich, and about his days of study and afterward. I'll pick up on this "Autumn Journal" where he's talking about how at Oxford—

> . . . it really was very attractive to be able to talk about tables
>   And to ask if the table *is*,
> And to draw the cork out of an old conundrum
>   And watch the paradoxes fizz.
> And it made one confident to think that nothing
>   Really was what it seemed under the sun,
> That the actual was not real and the real was not
>   with us
>   And all that mattered was the One . . .
> But certainly it was fun while it lasted
>   And I got my honours degree
> And was stamped as a person of intelligence and
>   culture
>   Forever wherever two or three
> Persons of intelligence and culture
>   Are gathered together in talk
> Writing definitions on invisible blackboards
>   In non-existent chalk.
> But such sacramental occasions
>   Are nowadays comparatively rare;
> There is always a wife or a boss or a dun or a
>   client
>   Disturbing the air.
> Barbarians always, life in the particular always,
>   Dozens of men in the street,
> And the perennial if unimportant problem
>   Of getting enough to eat.
> So blow the bugles over the metaphysicians,
>   Let the pure mind return to the Pure Mind;
> I must be content to remain in the world of
>   Appearance
>   And sit on the mere appearance of a behind.

But in case you should think my education was wasted
    I hasten to explain
That having once been to the university of Oxford
    You can never really again
Believe anything that anyone says and that of course
    is an asset
    In a world like ours;
Why bother to water a garden
    That is planted with paper flowers?
O the Freedom of the Press, the Late Night Final,
    To-morrow's pulp;
One should not gulp one's port but as it isn't
    Port, I'll gulp it if I want to gulp
But probably I'll just enjoy the colour
    And pour it down the sink
For I don't call advertisement a statement
    Or any quack medicine a drink.
Good-bye now, Plato and Hegel,
    The shop is closing down;
They don't want any philosopher-kings in England,
    There ain't no universals in this man's town.

I wrote this piece for a professional journal published by the Department of Philosophy and Fine Arts of the United States Air Force Academy.

MACHIAVELLI, MANAGEMENT, AND MORAL LEADERSHIP _____

United States Air Force Academy Journal of Professional Military Ethics, August 1982

Extortion, the squeeze-play drawing out of victims by force or compulsion, is dramatized in Godfather movies as an easily recognized explicit, usually illegal way of conducting business. In reality, though, it is conducted much more frequently in subtler ways—ways which are both more difficult to recognize and more difficult to deal with. And by no means are these ways illegal, at least not in the sense that I use the word. We frequently face extortionary pressures in our everyday life, for extortion is just a concentrated form of manipulation through the use of fear and guilt. We who are in hierarchies—be they academic, business, military, or some other sort—are always in positions in which people are trying to manipulate us, to get moral leverage on us. It is the wise leader who comes to the conclusion that he can't be had if he can't be made to feel guilty. That is as true today in a free environment as it was for me during my years in prison camp. You have got to keep yourself clean—never do or say anything of which you can be made to be ashamed—in order to avoid being manipulated. A smart man, an ethical man, never gives a manipulator an even break. He is always prepared to quench the extortionist's artful insinuation of guilt with the ice water of a truthful, clear-conscienced put-down. The more benign the environment, the more insidious is the extortionist's style. "Then Arthur learned," says the legend, "as all leaders are astonished to learn, that peace, not war, is the destroyer of men; that tranquility, rather than danger, is the mother of cowardice; and that not need, but plenty, brings apprehension and unease."

This is not to suggest that there is only one way to lead, one manner of leadership, one style that best fits all circumstances. Of course not. I have only said that all styles must be built on moral virtue. On specific leadership styles, I learned much from a talk by a psychoanalyst named Michael Maccoby. With a comprehensive understanding of American history, and after in-depth interviews of more than 200 American leaders of the 1970s, Maccoby concluded that there were four dominant leadership styles in the American past.

There are two things to remember as I quickly go over this analysis of Maccoby's. First of all, examples of men who embody each style have always been around and are still around; it's just that the challenges of different historic periods seemed to draw out particular types of leaders. And second, don't look for progress in leadership styles as we walk through this analysis. The leaders as leaders or as men don't get better as we follow the historic process.

From the Declaration of Independence until the credit system started to grow in the 1870s after the Civil War, most American leaders fell into a category he calls craftsmen. They were do-it-yourself guys: self-reliant, strong-willed, cautious, suspicious, harder on themselves than they are on others. Benjamin Franklin was cited as their prototype then, Aleksandr Solzhenitsyn now. Their target of competition was not other men, but rather their idea of their own potential. Craftsmen climbed ladders not to get ahead of others, but to achieve that level of excellence they believed they had within themselves. They were mountain climbers, not players of what systems analysts call zero sum games. They liked to make up their own minds; they did not buy school solutions. Craftsmen were men of conscience.

The industrial revolution and the need of its necessary credit and banking base were met by a new breed of leaders. Maccoby called them the jungle fighters. Jungle fighters played zero sum games with gusto; there was just so much business out there and these were the men who knew how to stake out territory and get it. Andrew Carnegie, the steel magnate, was the prototype. Like craftsmen, jungle fighters were also men of conscience. Although they could sit at the board of directors' table and figuratively decapitate incompetents with aplomb, they grieved. Characteristically they did not dodge issues; they settled scores eyeball to eyeball, tasting not only the self-satisfaction of authority but also the agony of pity.

After World War I, as the giant businesses the jungle fighters had built became bureaucracies, and as public relations grew into an everyday national preoccupation, those jungle fighters were gradually displaced by the smoother organization men. Like the jungle fighters, the organization men were paternalistic and authoritarian. But unlike those pioneers of industry and finance who were motivated primarily by competitive zeal, organization men, our psychoanalyst believes, were more motivated by a fear of failure. They were nevertheless characteristically honest; they were cautious men of conscience. They looked men in the eye when they fired them. They were men of the heart, possessing qualities with an emotional content: a sense of commitment, loyalty, humor, and spontaneity.

In the early 1960s, a fourth style emerged to take the prominent leadership role. Maccoby identifies practitioners of this style as the gamesmen. The gamesmen, impatient under the yoke of their paternalistic and authoritarian bosses, and educated more often than not in game-theory-oriented business schools, turned over a new page in leadership practices. The gamesmen believed that if one properly analyzes the game of life, the game of management, the game of leadership, one sees that it is not necessary to frame the problem as a zero sum game. Rather, in their minds, American life can be analyzed as a game in which any number can play and win.

These gamesmen were relaxed, objective, open-minded, detached, cerebral swingers. Such emotional baggage as commitment or conscience they deemed inefficient and unnecessary. "Play our cards rationally to win and go to bed and sleep like a baby without remorse." Some bothered with love and families; many gave them a tentative try and quit when they found them too burdensome. Maccoby said that there was a theatrical production that typified the leaders of each of these four ages and that the drama of the gamesmen was portrayed in the movie *The Sting*. You might remember that screenplay; in it, fair, competitive cooperative swingers, with the aid of teamwork and technology, destroyed the hung-up, authoritarian Godfather.

The gamesmen, concluded psychoanalyst Maccoby, were basically men of the head: cool intellectual types, walking calculating machines. Men of the head do many things well, but often have trouble coping with unpleasantness. These self-confident, cool, flexible men don't like to discipline people, they don't like to look people in the eye when they fire them. Moreover, they often crave to be loved, and that is a great leadership weakness. True leaders must be willing to stake out territory and identify and declare enemies. They must be fair and they may be compassionate, but they cannot be addicted to being loved by everybody. The man who has to be loved is an extortionist's dream. That man will do anything to avoid face-to-face unpleasantness; often he will sell his soul for praise. He can be had.

It was in the heyday of these gamesmen that some of their number, the so-called defense intellectuals took charge of the Pentagon under the direction of McNamara. At that juncture, I was fortunate enough to take a two-year sabbatical from military service for study at Stanford University. It was there that I started asking myself what truly rules the world: sentiment, efficiency, honor, justice?

The educated man, particularly the educated leader, copes with the fact that life is not fair. The problem for education is not to teach people how to deal with success but how to deal with failure. And the way to deal with failure is not to invent scapegoats or to lash out at your followers. Moreover, a properly educated leader, especially when harassed and under pressure, will know from his study of history and the classics that circumstances very much like those he is encountering have occurred from time to time on this earth since the beginning of history. He will avoid the self-indulgent error of seeing himself in a predicament so unprecedented, so unique, as to justify his making an exception to law, custom or morality in favor of himself. The making of such exceptions has been the theme of public life throughout much of our lifetimes. For twenty years, we've been surrounded by gamesmen unable to cope with the wisdom of the ages. They make exceptions to law and custom in favor of themselves because they choose to view ordinary dilemmas as unprecedented crises.

It has been generally toward the above issue that I directed a course at the Naval War College. My formula for attacking this problem with my student Lieutenant Colonels, Colonels, and Navy rank equivalents is the assignment of enough hard-core philosophy (the Book of Job, the Socratic dialogues of Plato, some of Aristotle's *Nichomachean Ethics*, Epictetus' *Enchiridion*, enough of Immanuel Kant to understand his concept of duty) and the reading of enough high-quality ultimate-situation literature (Feodor Dostoyevsky's *House of the Dead*, Albert Camus's *Plague*, Joseph Conrad's *Typhoon*, and Herman Melville's *Billy Budd*) as to deter self-pity when *in extremis*. With philosophy as the parent discipline, a discussion of courage might be focused on the writer who most thoroughly treated it, Aristotle. This might lead to the question of the validity of his viewpoint that courage is impossible in the absence of fear, that courage might be defined as a measure of how well one handles fear. How about the relationship between fear and imagination? Conrad has one of his characters state that imagination is the mother of fear. Must not a leader have imagination? If that breeds fear, might that not sap his courage? He surely must have courage above all else . . . etc. From such readings and discussions come understandings and clarifications of those elements of leadership which served in antiquity and those which must serve now.

Leadership must be based on goodwill. Goodwill does not mean posturing and, least of all, pandering to the mob. It means obvious and wholehearted commitment to helping followers. We are tired of leaders we fear, tired of leaders we love, and most tired of leaders who let us take liberties with them. What we need for leaders are men of the heart who are so helpful that they, in effect, do away with the need of their jobs. But leaders like that are never out of a job, never out of followers. Strange as it sounds, great leaders gain authority by giving it away.

I am firmly convinced that the time I spent at Stanford has been a major force in molding my own personality as a leader. And I am just as firmly convinced that education in the classics and in the principles of human relationships gave me far better preparation for being a prisoner of war than did the traditional survival and evasion training. My ideas on the art of moral leadership received their most profound testing in the stress and degradation—yes, in the extortion environment—of a Communist prisoner of war camp.

The intensity and stark drama of my eight years in North Vietnam provided a quantity and range of leadership challenge that would more than fill an ordinary lifetime. In mere months or weeks, men made and destroyed their reputations. Those behind bars seemed to be scanning reams of data on the problems of good and evil in fast time. The extortion system, powered by our enemy's willingness to torture and impose isolation, quickly drove to the surface issues of moral integrity which at the pace of normal life could take years to fester and erupt into public view.

For united resistance, men had to get on quickly with the business of assimilating knowledge of the character traits of their fellow prisoners. This knowledge had to be more penetrating and more calculating than the sort commonly found sufficient for amicable social life out here in freedom. Is the newcomer emotionally stable? (We had to make a good guess as to whether he had the steadfastness and composure to warrant being trusted with secret material in that torture environment.) Does he have moral integrity? In the privacy of the torture room, will he go to the wall in silence, or do what is so commonplace in the business world nowadays and try to make a deal? Is he sophisticated enough to avoid falling for the interrogator's bait? Will he work his way out on a limb by gabbing after that clever interrogator has dangled before him such American-life enticements as: Let us reason together; you are a pragmatic people, meet us halfway?

In the extortion environment one can always better his own position at the expense of his fellows by holding still for the manipulator's setting up of subtle compromises. A loner makes out by making acknowledged or tacit deals. This will never do. The intensity of life in jail clearly illuminated for us prisoners of war the truth that for the greatest good for the greatest number of us, for our maximum happiness, maximum self-respect, maximum protection of one another, each of us had to submerge our individual survival instincts into an ideal of universal solidarity. "No deals" and "Unity over self" became our mottoes.

Some of you are doubtless skeptical of the practicability of such ideals which seem to ask more of a man than human nature might be thought to allow. To the skeptics let me say right off that when there is leadership by example, and when there is a commonly shared threat of total estrangement and humiliation, united magnanimous behavior can become a reality. When a man looks through creeping and growing fissures in the thin veneer of civilization that coats his existence, he suddenly realizes that his slip back into barbarism could come about in weeks. As he peers over the edge of his world, it dawns on him how lonesome and terrible it would be down there without communication, friends, or common cultural ties. He vividly realizes how men, fellow countrymen, need one another for understanding and for sanity. As he sees himself clinging to a receding civilization with his fingernails, it becomes clear to him that "No deals" and "Unity over self" are not goody-goody idealist slogans; rather they are practical guides to action.

We saw that we had to build and tend our own civilization if we were to keep ourselves from becoming animals. A man must relate to a community, a commonality of communication style, a commonality of ritual, of laws, of traditions, of poetry, of shared dreams, if he is to prevail, if he is to resist. "Man does not live by bread alone." Learning the truth and full meaning of that biblical adage was lesson one for us in that crucible of pressure.

It goes without saying that the first job of leadership is to provide the communication necessary for that civilization, that ritual, those laws, those traditions. The problem was to improvise a communications system for a prison camp in which everybody lived in solitary confinement, a solitary confinement in silence, a solitary confinement in which torture was inevitable for those who break that silence to communicate with their fellows. Our Vietnam enemies gave us two ways to go on this. We could lie low and not communicate and go to seed over the years of silence and solitude. (One starts "looking for a friend" after a couple of years.) Or we could communicate as a matter of duty and take our lumps. Since the dictates of conscience and morality made the latter the only way to go, the problem became how to communicate stealthily. For us, trapped in isolation in Hanoi, the means for that communication was a tap code that would break through the walls of solitary confinement, the walls of silence. (For the mechanics of the code, I suggest reading Commander Everett Alvarez's "Sound: A POW's Weapon," pages 91–93, in the August 1976 *Proceedings*. See also Section II of these essays.)

Leadership basics are vividly portrayed in the prison camp example. Prison serves as a useful test bed (to use a test pilot expression) in which to study in detail man's behavior under stress, stress of the sort under which many of life's crucial decisions are necessarily made. Mark this down in your book as lesson two: in the high-stress situation, status will not carry you as a leader. That is to say, you have to have more going for you than your title, your seniority, your position in your hierarchy, your rank. You cannot get by with performing like a quarterback who is functional only while being protected in the pocket; you've got to be able to scramble and improvise, on your feet, and alone. Even this assumes that by the time the pressure is on, you would have earned your followers' respect, and not just their fear or friendship. Unless people respect you as a leader, when the fat is in the fire they'll just listen to your orders and calmly walk away.

Lesson three: Under stress, ordinary transactional leadership will never cut it. That is to say, transactional leadership propelled simply by the effect of give and take, leadership driven by the base instincts of the marketplace and bargaining table whereby the leader makes an accommodation in the expectation that his followers will make a complementary accommodation, simply will not stand up. This may come as news to you because the transactional leader/follower relationship is so much a part of our way of doing business in everyday economic, social, even academic life. But what to us is the ordinary dance of life, the dance propelled by continuous compromise finds itself floundering under pressure. Inputs are needed from *transforming* leaders. Transforming leaders don't simply analyze what they think their people want and then try to give them part of it and hope they will receive a counter-accommodation in return. Transforming leaders instruct and inspire their followers to recognize worthy needs, and they make those needs their wants. They have a way of raising their followers out of their everyday selves and into their better selves, of making them conscious of the high-minded goals that lie unconscious beneath their self-centered desires. The transforming leader has the wisdom to read the minds of his flock, to understand what they want, to know what they ought to want, and the persuasive power to implant the latter into their hearts.

In all that I have been saying, I've made the points that leaders under pressure must keep themselves absolutely clean morally (the relativism of the social sciences will never do). They must lead by example, must be able to implant high-mindedness in their followers, must have competence beyond status, and must have earned their followers' respect by demonstrating integrity. What I've been describing as the necessary leadership attributes under pressure are the bedrock virtues all successful leaders must possess, under pressure and otherwise. Prison was just the test bed, just the meat grinder that tore away everything else, leaving only these bones to hold me in place.

This letter to the editor closes the loop that was opened by my "Back From Hanoi" article written ten years earlier. As I look at them side by side, it seems to me that time has heightened, rather than mellowed, my anger at the squander of our national substance, the lives of our soldiers, and our national fortune in a war run like an exercise in game theory. I leave the experience behind me wishing not that we will cover up the truth ("heal the wounds of Vietnam," as the popular expression goes), but that we will never allow ourselves to forget the penalties extracted by halfhearted and softheaded national leadership in matters involving the very serious enterprise of the use of combat arms.

SPECIAL CORRESPONDENCE ―――――

The American Spectator, June 1983

Dear Mr. Tyrrell,

Thank you for your letter of January 19, and your agreeable comments about my appearance with Diane Sawyer on CBS morning news on January 13. She was a peach, and it was a pleasure to be led in such a relaxed manner through a brief discussion of my experiences as a prisoner of war in Hanoi, and to chat with her about the academic course I'm teaching at Stanford.

But did you catch that same show at the same time exactly two weeks later? Diane Sawyer was not part of that 7:45 segment on January 27; rather for about five minutes the screen was filled with old Vietnam war scenes narrated off camera by Bill McLaughlin. He reminded viewers that January 27 was the tenth anniversary of the signing of the Vietnam Peace Accords:

> . . . and then [on December 18, 1972] came the Christmas bombing of civilian targets . . . which had nothing to do with ending the war . . . The number of civilian casualties has yet to be released.

There are enough falsehoods in that paragraph alone to justify a demand for equal time. Those eleven days of bombing at the end of 1972 are a subject I could discuss on CBS morning news with *real* credentials. I was an eyewitness. And the truth is that not one bomb was dropped on Christmas; civilian targets were never deliberately hit (and far fewer were accidentally hit than in any bombing of a large industrial complex since the invention of the airplane); the raids broke the will of the North Vietnamese as did nothing else in that war; and the number of total casualties (some lesser part of which were undoubtedly civilians) was publicly released by the North Vietnamese government and printed in the *New York Times* within a week after the last bomb was dropped on December 29. The casualty number was extremely low—1,318 killed—no more than a scant percentage of the casualty numbers common for European and Japanese cities bombed with comparable tonnage during World War II. Moreover, North Vietnam persisted, and still persists, in the validity of their figures. These facts have been in the public domain for years, yet they have been ignored again and again and again. So let me make a few points you won't normally hear on CBS.

If I learned nothing else during eight years in wartime Hanoi, it was that Clausewitz is as right today as he was during the Napoleonic Wars; the name of the game in war is to break the enemy's *will*.

Now airpower's greatest utility is its shock effect, its ability to create fear and panic, particularly among the uninitiated and undisciplined. By the time our tactical raids crept up to Hanoi in 1966, every civilian in the city had undergone months and months of instruction in civil defense. "The scenario goes like this," the party cadre's man might well have explained to the people on his block: "The aid-raid siren wails in midmorning, you run and get in your hole, the planes roll in, there is a lot of noise, a bridge is bombed, the 'all clear' is sounded. By then there are a few fires and the trucks wheel past; there are also likely to be a few casualties, particularly at the anti-aircraft batteries, and one or two ambulances might be heard en route. Meanwhile, the other 99.99 percent of us can chop chop by the numbers back to our work stations. And that's all there is to it until afternoon when it will all start and end within fifteen minutes just like it did in the morning."

City life can seemingly go on forever under mere tactical bombings if the population is well indoctrinated. (Bloomington could cope, too, with prior instruction like this.)

In Hanoi in those years of tactical bombings, there were few surprises. Everything seemed programmed. The Americans were constrained by self-imposed rules that were public knowledge on the streets of North Vietnam's capital city. Though the guards of the prisons feigned wide-eyed hostility during the few minutes of the raid, the street sounds were back to normal right after the all clear siren. Patriotic music was soon blaring from the speakers at every corner, while our interrogators strutted about the prison yards defiantly. By nightfall an almost carnival atmosphere could be sensed. Songfests went off as scheduled in the guards' quarters and in the city parks. Clever American prisoners with a good ear for lyrics could identify the targets hit that day from their mention in songs sung that night.

Thus went life in Hanoi throughout the latter half of 1966, all of 1967, and through March of 1968—until President Johnson halted the bombing. In Hanoi, this stoppage brought about no change in the brutality with which we prisoners were treated. For many of us, our very worst tortures occurred during that Johnson-initiated hiatus of bombing. Our North Vietnamese captors seemed contemptuous of our government's sheepishness.

In late 1971 in Hanoi we began to hear air raid sirens again, and a new generation of prisoners started to trickle in to join us. Off and on for about a year, we had the tactical raid situation we had known five and six years before.

But a totally contrasting atmosphere swept the city about an hour after dark on that December 18 night in 1972. At first we (in the very center of Hanoi in Hoa Lo prison) thought it was a regular tactical raid of the sort that came in every few nights. The bombs were hitting out where they usually hit—in the railroad yards, power plant, and airfield areas. Some of the prisoners did detect higher level explosions early in the bombardment, but it wasn't until these explosions were still being heard 20 minutes later that the cheers started to go up all over the cell blocks of that downtown prison. This was a new reality for Hanoi. These were big explosions—and the bombs kept coming! Though landing thousands of yards away, they shook the ground under us and plaster fell from all the ceilings. The days of Mickey Mouse were over! Our wonderful America was here to deliver a message, not a self-conscious stammer of apology. "Let's hear it for President Nixon!" went the cry from cell block to cell block, all around the courtyard.

And the bombers kept coming, and we kept cheering. Guards, normally enraged by loud talk, guards who normally thrust their bayonetted rifles through the bars and screamed at us if we had the temerity to shout, could only be seen silently cowering in the lee of the prison walls, their faces ashen in the light reflected from the fiery skies above.

So it went, hour after hour, night after night, with frequent tactical raids in the daytime. Once in a while, prisoners on the far side of the compound, looking south, identified a particularly brilliant torch among the array of bursting antiaircraft shells and surface-to-air missiles. Some claimed they could then make out a tumbling, burning B-52. But if they could see one, all Hanoi could see it too. For the North Vietnamese to see that and the bomber stream continuing to roll right on like Old Man River was a message in itself: proof that all that separated Hanoi from doomsday was an American national order to keep the bombs out on the hard targets. We prisoners knew this was the end of North Vietnamese resistance, and the North Vietnamese knew it, too.

At dawn, the streets of Hanoi were absolutely silent. The usual patriotic wakeup music was missing, the familiar street sounds, the horns, all gone. In prison, interrogators and guards would inquire about our needs solicitously. Unprecedented morning coffee was delivered to our cell blocks. One look at any Vietnamese officer's face told the whole story. It telegraphed accommodation, hopelessness, remorse, fear. The shock was there; our enemy's will was broken. The sad thing was that we all knew that what we were seeing could have been done in any ten-day period in the previous seven years and saved the lives of thousands, including most of those 58,000 dead Americans.

By December 29, Hanoi was almost out of ammunition. (The mining of Haiphong harbor worked, too.) There was no need to continue the bombing. The North Vietnamese negotiators (who had come home to Hanoi in a huff just before the B-52s rolled in on December 18) were anxious to rejoin Henry Kissinger at the conference table. In less than two weeks they accepted our terms. And in less than a month I was back in Coronado, California, with my wife, Sybil, and our four kids to whom I had said goodbye eight years before.

James Bond Stockdale
Hoover Institution
Stanford, California

ABOUT THE AUTHOR _____

Vice Admiral James Bond Stockdale was a true American hero. Shot down on September 9, 1965, during a mission over North Vietnam, he spent seven and a half years as a prisoner of war. Despite enduring relentless torture, intimidation, and four years of solitary confinement, he refused to capitulate, even earning the grudging respect of his captors. He ultimately received 26 combat decorations, including two Distinguished Flying Crosses, three Distinguished Service Medals, four Silver Star Medals, two Purple Hearts, and the Congressional Medal of Honor, the nation's highest award for valor. He had the distinction of being the only three-star officer in the history of the navy to wear both aviator wings and the Medal of Honor.

Stockdale retired from the military in 1979 to become president of the Citadel, a widely renowned military college in South Carolina. On his retirement, the navy established the Vice Admiral James Bond Stockdale Leadership Award, which is presented annually to two commanding officers, one in the Atlantic Fleet and one in the Pacific Fleet.

He left the Citadel in 1981 to become a senior research fellow at the Hoover Institution at Stanford University. In addition to this book, he is the author of two other works published by Hoover Institution: *Courage under Fire: Testing Epictetus's Doctrines in a Laboratory of Human Behavior* (Hoover Essays, No. 6, 1993) and *Reflections of a Philosophical Fighter Pilot* (1995). Stockdale and his wife, Sybil, were coauthors of *In Love and War* (Harper & Row, 1984), which in 1987 was made into an NBC television movie viewed by more than 45 million Americans.

In 1992 Admiral Stockdale was an independent candidate for vice president of the United States as Ross Perot's running mate. He said he ran to repay his debt to Perot, who had worked to help free POWs in Vietnam.

In 1993 Stockdale became the first naval aviator of the Vietnam era to be inducted into the Carrier Aviation Hall of Fame. He was later the subject of *Stockdale Triumphs: A Return to Vietnam*, a documentary about his first trip back to Vietnam in 1994. Produced by Catherine O'Brien of the Stanford Video Media Group, the film received a Telly Award in the history/biography category. In the 45-minute video, he returns to Hanoi and the Hoa Lo prison—the "Hanoi Hilton"—where he was held for most of his imprisonment, discussing his prisoner of war experience and exploring the changed city.

James B. Stockdale died at his home in Coronado, California, in 2005 at the age of 81. At the time of his death he held eleven honorary doctoral degrees. His home, where he lived since 1963, has been designated a city landmark.

CPSIA information can be obtained
at www.ICGtesting.com
Printed in the USA
LVHW051535090123
736779LV00004B/736